Interpreting
the Pauline Epistles

Guides to New Testament Exegesis
Scot McKnight, General Editor

Interpreting the Pauline Epistles

Thomas R. Schreiner

BAKER BOOK HOUSE
Grand Rapids, Michigan 49516

Copyright © 1990 by Baker Books
a division of Baker Book House Company
P.O. Box 6287, Grand Rapids, MI 49516-6287

ISBN: 0-8010-8302-8

Fourth printing, January 1998

Printed in the United States of America

Library of Congress Cataloging-in-Publication Data

Schreiner, Thomas R.
    Interpreting the Pauline Epistles / Thomas R. Schreiner.
        p.   cm. — (Guides to New Testament exegesis ; 5)
    Includes bibliographical references and index.
    ISBN 0-8010-8302-8
    1. Bible. N.T. Epistles of Paul—Criticism, interpretation, etc.
  I. Title. II. Series.
  BS2650.2.S36   1990
  227'.061—dc20   90-45013
                                                  CIP

For information about academic books, resources for
Christian leaders, and all new releases available from
Baker Book House, visit our web site:
                http://www.bakerbooks.com/

To my wife
Diane,
my fellow-heir
in the greatest cause.

Contents

Editor's Preface

Four literary types (genres) comprise the New Testament: the Gospels, the Acts of the Apostles, the Letters, and, finally, the Apocalypse. Each genre is distinct, and, as has been made abundantly clear by contemporary scholars, each requires different sensitivities, principles, and methods of interpretation. Consequently, applying the same method to different genres will often lead to serious misunderstandings. Consequently, students need manuals that will introduce them both to the specific nature of a particular genre and to basic principles for exegeting that genre.

The Guides to New Testament Exegesis series has been specifically designed to meet this need. These guides have been written, not for specialists, but for college religion majors, seminarians, and pastors who have had at least one year of Greek. Methods and principles may change, but the language of the New Testament remains the same. God chose to speak to people in Greek; serious students of the New Testament must learn to love that language in order better to understand the Word of God.

These guides also have a practical aim. Each guide presents various views of scholars on particular issues. Yet the ultimate goal of each is to provide methods and principles for interpreting the New Testament. Abstract discussions have their proper place but not in this series; these guides are intended for concrete application to the New Testament text. Various scholars, specializing in given areas of New Testament study, offer students their own methods and principles for interpreting specific genres of the New Testament. Such diversity provides a broader perspective for the student. Each volume concludes with a bibliography of twenty essential works for further study.

Previously the point was made that different genres require different methods and principles. A basic exegetical method which can be adapted to various genres, however, is also essential. Because of the inevitable overlap of procedures, an introductory volume to the series covers the basic methods and principles for each genre. The individual exegetical guides will then introduce the student to more specific background procedures for that particular genre.

The vision for this series comes from Gordon Fee's introduction to New Testament exegesis.[1] Without minimizing the important contribution Fee has made to New Testament study, this series goes beyond what he has presented. It intends to develop, as it were, handbooks for each of the genres of the New Testament.[2]

Finally, this series is dedicated to our teachers and students, in thanksgiving and hope. Our prayer is that God may use these books to lead his people into truth, love, and peace.

Scot McKnight

1. *New Testament Exegesis: A Handbook for Students and Pastors* (Philadelphia: Westminster, 1983).

2. A helpful introduction to the various genres of the New Testament is D. E. Aune, *The New Testament in Its Literary Environment*, Library of Early Christianity (Philadelphia: Westminster, 1987).

Preface

Writing a book makes one very conscious that no book is ever written by one person alone. I am grateful to the general editor, Scot McKnight, for inviting me to contribute this book to the series and for his thoughtful comments on earlier editions of the work. His criticisms were always penetrating and kind. My colleague at Bethel, Robert Stein, read the entire manuscript with his usual care and saved me from many errors. Another colleague, James Brooks, read my chapters on textual criticism and diagramming, providing invaluable advice on each.

Tom Steller, one of my pastors at Bethlehem Baptist Church, has been not only a friend who displays the warmth and gentleness of Christ, but he also taught me how to trace the argument of a passage (see the method described in chapter six). A special thanks is due to Dan Fuller of Fuller Seminary, for the method used in chapter six ultimately comes from him. He also gave me the permission to disseminate it in this book. I also benefitted from his system of diagramming. Dan read the chapters on diagramming and tracing the argument with an eagle eye so that he detected many problems, and helped make this book much better than it would have been otherwise. I should say, however, that I have not followed all of his advice, and thus any errors in those chapters should be laid solely at my feet.

It was a joy to work with my editor from Baker, Gary Knapp. He improved the book in countless ways for which I

11

am grateful. This book also evinces a dependence upon my mentor from Fuller Seminary, Don Hagner. His *New Testament Theology and Exegesis* class influenced me significantly, and the annotated notebook he has compiled has been consulted again and again. Mark Reasoner, a colleague at Bethel College, read about half the manuscript, and I have incorporated some of his insightful suggestions, especially in regard to bibliographic material. I do want to say, and not just for perfunctory reasons, that any shortcomings in the book are mine alone. None of the people mentioned above would agree with everything said in this book, and yet all of them have made this book better than it would otherwise be.

My final and most important thanks are extended to my wife Diane. She constantly reminds me that biblical scholarship is "a noisy gong and clanging cymbal" if the church of Christ is not edified. She and my three boys, Daniel, Patrick, and John, often drew me away from this book, not by nagging me but by delighting me with their own joy of life and joy in God. To Him be the glory!

Introduction

Since 13 of the 27 books in the NT are attributed to Paul, a separate book on how to do Pauline exegesis is warranted.[1] Moreover, the importance of Pauline exegesis is evident from the crucial role Pauline theology has played in the history of the church. It was Pauline theology that had such a major influence on Augustine, Luther, Calvin, and Barth. Any contemporary theology that endeavors to be rooted in and faithful to biblical revelation must wrestle hard and long with Pauline exegesis.

One of the issues we must tackle in this book, therefore, is how we move from exegesis to constructing a Pauline theology. Interpreters inevitably move from exegesis to theology, but it is imperative that such theologizing is truly rooted in exegesis. Furthermore, if Paul's theology is seen to be normative and authoritative for today's world (as I think it is), then the issue of significance arises. Accordingly, we ask: How should we apply Paul's theology to our culture today? How do we translate Paul's word to the 20th-century world? We must be ever mindful that the process of exegesis is not complete unless we bridge the gap between the 1st-century world and the contemporary world. These questions are thorny hermeneutical issues that we will examine in a later chapter.

1. For some other recent introductory works on the Pauline letters, see L. E. Keck and V. P. Furnish, *The Pauline Letters* (Nashville: Abingdon, 1984); C. J. Roetzel, *The Letters of Paul: Conversations in Context*, 2d ed. (Atlanta: John Knox, 1982); M. L. Soards, *The Apostle Paul: An Introduction to His Writings and Teaching* (New York: Paulist, 1987); M. D. Hooker, *A Preface to Paul* (New York: Oxford University Press, 1980); E. E. Ellis, *Paul and His Recent Interpreters* (Grand Rapids: Eerdmans, 1961).

The importance of doing Pauline exegesis is evident from the above comments, but any discussion of Pauline theology and the significance of his word for today is premature. First, we must study the nuts and bolts of Pauline exegesis. Now some overlap exists between how we do Pauline exegesis and how we do exegesis in the rest of the NT. For instance, textual criticism operates on the same basic principles in Paul as elsewhere, even though different MSS may be superior in Paul than in the Synoptics. Thus, instead of repeating the basic principles of textual criticism found elsewhere in handbooks on exegetical methodology, this book shall highlight a couple of distinctives for doing textual criticism in the Pauline corpus and give several examples. Likewise, the basic methodology used in lexical studies is not unique in Paul, and so we will not restate the general principles required in studying words. But we shall try to unfold some of the issues in lexical study by focusing on specific examples.

One of the distinguishing features of Pauline literature is the difference in genre. Paul did not write Gospels, nor did he write a history of the early church like Acts, nor did he even write an apocalyptic work like Revelation. He wrote letters to specific communities and individuals. The exegete must take into account the difference in genre when he or she interprets the Pauline letters. To interpret letters as we do narrative or apocalyptic literature would be to miss the genius of what is involved in the letters. The fact that Paul wrote letters gives us two more areas to consider: (1) we need to understand what makes epistolary literature distinctive in order to interpret Paul's letters accurately; (2) Paul wrote these letters in history, and so some comprehension of introductory and historical questions is essential. The more we know about the particular circumstances of a letter, and the history and culture of the time in which Paul wrote the letter, the better we will understand that letter.

Paul's letters also differ from narrative in that they contain highly involved syntax and tightly constructed arguments. This is an oversimplification since some parts of the Gospels and Acts (e.g., Luke 1:1–4) are syntactically complex and contain involved and intricate arguments. Indeed, carefully constructed arguments are especially evident in the speeches found in the Gospels and Acts. Yet all NT scholars recognize that involved syntax and careful argumentation are distinctive features of Pauline literature. For instance, Ephesians 1:3–14 is a single sentence in Greek. Not only does Paul write long sentences, but his arguments are sustained and ongoing, with each chapter building upon the previous one. This is not to say that narrative literature has no structure, for it certainly does. Whereas narrative displays structure that is portrayed primarily by the selection of events and speeches, Paul's letters display a more argumentative structure.

Since the Pauline letters are grammatically involved and logically complex, diagramming and tracing the argument become particularly important in order to unravel his syntax and unfold his argument. There are no easy shortcuts for understanding Paul. The exegete can grasp the meaning of Paul's letters only through patient attention to syntax and disciplined thinking about the argument of the text. Thus we need to spend a chapter each on the topics of diagramming and tracing the argument of Pauline letters.

Much of what we say about the Pauline letters will also apply to the other letters of the NT. Nevertheless, the Pauline letters present unique challenges in distinction from all other epistolary literature in the NT. The reason for this is the fact that we have 13 letters that are ascribed to Paul, and no other writer even comes close to this number. The distinctiveness of interpreting Paul is especially prominent theologically because his theology must be extrapolated from 13 letters and not just one or two.

The various topics mentioned above afford the reader some idea of what we must study in order to interpret the Pauline letters. But these areas of study were not discussed in a logical order. The list below itemizes nine areas of study in the order in which we shall investigate them in this book (notice that the list corresponds to the chapter divisions in this book).

Understanding the Nature of Letters
Doing Textual Criticism
Translating and Analyzing the Letter
Investigating Historical and Introductory Issues
Diagramming and Conducting a Grammatical Analysis
Tracing the Argument

Doing Lexical Studies
Probing the Theological Context
Delineating the Significance of Paul's Letters

The rest of this chapter will set forth certain assumptions about the nature of exegesis and the motivation for exegesis. What is said below applies to the exegesis of all Scripture, and not just the Pauline letters. I am deeply conscious of the fact that the hermeneutical issues addressed here cry out for more detailed discussion and defense. Nevertheless, these issues need to be touched on briefly, for exegesis is never done in a vacuum. Indeed, more in-depth analysis is also needed for many of the other issues addressed in this book, particularly those in the last two chapters on Pauline theology and the significance of Paul's letters for today. Detailed discussions of these matters, however, would require a book on almost every issue broached, a task that lies beyond the scope of this work if it is to remain a handbook on Pauline exegesis.

Ultimate Goal of Exegesis

I have often wondered why biblical exegesis is not the consuming passion of pastors and students. Why is it, for example, that so many sermons have very little to do with what the biblical text is saying? Undoubtedly there are various reasons for such a state of affairs. I want to focus on only one reason here. Biblical exegesis is often neglected by students and pastors because they consider it to be the special province of biblical scholars, and the debates that biblical scholars engage in are not considered to be relevant to the life of the ordinary person. Some people consider biblical scholars to be specialists who investigate and debate issues that have very little to do with practical everyday living. Sadly enough, scholars share some of the blame here, for they have often failed to see or to share the wider implications of their work. They have become specialists. So the ordinary person asks: Why should I learn any more about the labyrinth of NT scholarship than about the latest research on astronomy? Reading the latest theories in astronomy may be intellectually stimulating but it is deemed to be practically useless. So too students often relegate biblical exegesis to the scholarly shelf and abandon it as soon as they complete their academic course work.

Evangelicals have too often responded to the world of scholarship with an anti-intellectual attitude. Recognizing the glaring deficiencies of critical scholarship, evangelicals have sometimes responded by denying the need for critical and searching study of the Bible.[2] In lieu of serious study some segments of the evangelical subculture have trumpeted a somewhat naive and simplistic way of understanding Scripture. Erasmus long ago revealed the error of such a mind-set with this penetrating remark: "People say to me, How can scholarly knowledge facilitate the understanding of Holy Scripture? My answer is, How does ignorance contribute to it?"[3]

But how can we convince students that studying Scripture is not merely for the purpose of attaining excellence in a specialized discipline? Of course we need specialists who intensively study a particular subject, but the goal of exegesis is not to gain specialized knowledge in a particular field of study. The goal of exegesis is to gain a worldview based upon and informed by the biblical text. Ultimately, we all conduct our lives based on our worldview, our perception of life as a whole. Biblical exegesis should be the foundation in the building of that worldview. The complete building is ultimately expressed in our systematic theology, for systematic theology is another way of speaking of one's worldview. Someone has rightly said that every Christian has a systematic theology. The question is this: Is the systematic theology faithful to the biblical text and logically rigorous, or is it contrary to the biblical text and logically in disarray?

One of the problems in the contemporary world is that many biblical scholars do not believe that it is possible to

2. The word "critical" does not mean that the reader stands in judgment over the Bible. It means that the reader's understanding of Scripture is based on informed and intelligent judgments. All people make judgments regarding the meaning of the biblical text. The question is whether those judgments are intelligent, plausible, and cogent.

3. Cited in D. B. Lockerbie, "A Call for Christian Humanism," *Bibliotheca Sacra* 143 (1986): 20. For a penetrating analysis regarding the state of the study of Scripture among Evangelicals, see S. J. Hafemann, "Seminary, Subjectivity, and the Centrality of Scripture: Reflections on the Current Crisis in Evangelical Seminary Education," *Journal of the Evangelical Theological Society* 31 (1988): 129–143.

derive a coherent worldview or systematic theology from the biblical text. In so doing, however, such scholars are seemingly undermining the very enterprise in which they are engaged.[4] A few intellectuals will always want to continue the tradition of biblical scholarship, but the ordinary person will soon recognize that biblical exegesis is not vital for the formation of a worldview in the 20th century if the documents do not communicate a coherent message. No one can base his or her life on documents that are inconsistent in their message. Biblical theologians often warn of the dangers of a systematic theology not based on the text but on the pernicious practice of prooftexting, and they are correct in doing so since all systematic theology should be informed by and based on solid exegesis.[5] Students will relish the study of exegesis if they regard it as the foundation of a grand vision. Yet if exegesis is simply considered to be expertise in a very specialized discipline, only a few will be interested, but the majority will ignore acquiring the tools needed to practice this discipline.

Exegesis will not be the passion of students unless they see that it plays a vital role in the formation of one's worldview. An intellectual inclination for exegesis, although crucial, is not sufficient. Exegesis will never be one's *passion* unless one's heart is gripped by biblical truth; only then will it lead to a deeper and richer joy in God (John 15:11). If one's heart never sings when doing exegesis, then the process has not reached its culmination. And if one has never trembled when doing exegesis (Isa. 66:2), then one is not listening for the voice of God.

Of course, the renewal of our minds and the flaming of the heart are designed to lead to obedience, to a change in the way we live, to the approving of the perfect will of God in our experience (Rom. 12:2). And not only that, a person who has been transformed by the biblical text will want to share the truth that has changed him or her with others. Like the

4. For a very helpful discussion of the possibility and importance of systematic theology in exegesis, see D. A. Carson, "Unity and Diversity in the New Testament: The Possibility of Systematic Theology," in *Scripture and Truth*, ed. D. A. Carson and J. D. Woodbridge (Grand Rapids: Zondervan, 1983), 65–95.

5. For an example of the melding together of exegesis and systematic theology, see S. L. Johnson, Jr., "Romans 5:12—An Exercise in Exegesis and Theology," in *New Dimensions in New Testament Study*, ed. R. N. Longenecker and M. C. Tenney (Grand Rapids: Zondervan, 1974), 281–97.

Servant of the Lord we will be taught "to know the word that sustains the weary" (Isa. 50:4). We will communicate these truths to "reliable men who will also be qualified to teach others" (2 Tim. 2:2).

To sum up: Exegesis is part of the process of building one's worldview, and as one sees the truth it inflames one's heart and constrains one to live a new life and to pass this new truth on to others. Thereby, the kingdom of God advances, and God is glorified.

Assumptions in Forming a Worldview

Two assumptions are implicit in what I have written above and they should be made explicit. First, we cannot build a worldview from Scripture unless the Scriptures present a unified worldview. If the Scriptures are contradictory in what they teach, then we cannot derive a coherent worldview from them. Here I assume that the Scriptures do present a coherent and consistent worldview, but such an assertion will not be defended in detail here.[6]

Second, I assume the law of noncontradiction to be foundational for one's view of truth. The law of noncontradiction is not just a Western conception of truth. If we dispense with the law of noncontradiction, then all rational discussion is impossible.[7] For example, if we claim that what James and Paul teach about justification is actually contradictory, that is, James and Paul do not mean different things by the words *faith* and *works*, but rather they affirm two different and mutually exclusive ways of justification, then the only rational conclusion is that they contradict each other. And if they do contradict, then the Bible ceases to be authoritative on the issue of justification since it teaches no consistent view. Whether we prefer Paul or James will primarily be a matter of our subjective preference. And if Scripture is contradictory in

6. For a nuanced definition of inerrancy, see P. D. Feinberg, "The Meaning of Inerrancy," in *Inerrancy*, ed. N. L. Geisler (Grand Rapids: Zondervan, 1979), 267–304. For a defense of the coherency and accuracy of Scripture, see C. F. H. Henry, *God, Revelation and Authority*, 4 vols. (Waco: Word, 1976–79).

7. For a brief defense of the law of noncontradiction, see N. L. Geisler, "Philosophical Presuppositions of Biblical Errancy," in *Inerrancy*, ed. N. L. Geisler (Grand Rapids: Zondervan, 1979), 308–10, and D. A. Carson, "Unity and Diversity," 80–81.

one place, there is no reason *in principle* why it could not be contradictory in others as well. Now we could give good reasons for the complementary nature of Paul's and James' views of justification. But the point here is simply this: in this book I will assume that Scripture is consistent and that it does not contradict itself.

Definition of Exegesis and the Intention of the Author

Exegesis is the method by which we ascertain what an author meant when he or she wrote a particular piece of literature. The meaning of Scripture cannot be separated from the intention of the author as that intention is expressed in the words of the text.[8] We assume that we can discover the meaning that is intended by the human authors of Scripture. We reject, therefore, any theory that says that the meaning of the author is unattainable or that the reader imposes one's own meaning onto the text.

It is also incorrect to say that our goal is to discover *God's* intention in the biblical text rather than the intention of the human author. We aim to discover God's meaning, but such a meaning cannot be known apart from the intention of the human author.[9] God has so designed it that his meaning is known when the meaning of the human author is known. If we claim that God's intention in the text is not the same as that of the human author, how can we substantiate or demonstrate God's intention in the text? Each person would subjectively determine the meaning of the text. Any normativity of meaning would be excluded a priori since the discussion of

8. For a defense of interpreting literature in accordance with authorial intent, see E. D. Hirsch, Jr., *Validity in Interpretation* (New Haven: Yale University Press, 1967), and *Aims in Interpretation* (Chicago: University of Chicago Press, 1976). Although sympathetic with Hirsch, P. D. Juhl (*Interpretation* [Princeton: Princeton University Press, 1980]) rightly criticized some weaknesses in Hirsch's analysis, and, in fact, provided an even more cogent defense of authorial intent than Hirsch did. See also K. J. Vanhoozer ("A Lamp in the Labyrinth: The Hermeneutics of 'Aesthetic' Theology," *Trinity Journal* 88 [1987]: 25–56) for a nuanced and recent defense of authorial intent.

9. See D. P. Fuller, "The Holy Spirit's Role in Biblical Interpretation," in *Scripture, Tradition, and Interpretation*, ed. W. W. Gasque and W. S. LaSor (Grand Rapids: Eerdmans, 1978), 189–98. D. J. Moo ("The Problem of *Sensus Plenior*," in *Hermeneutics, Authority, and Canon*, ed. D. A. Carson and J. D. Woodbridge [Grand Rapids: Zondervan, 1986], 179–211) thought that there may be a fuller sense in the OT texts, and that a canonical approach can yield a fuller sense than that intended by the OT author.

the meaning of the text would no longer depend upon the diction, grammar, and syntax of the human author.

The Role of Preunderstanding in Exegesis

Most scholars now agree that exegesis without presuppositions is impossible.[10] We are all shaped by our culture and background. Many of our presuppositions are helpful and valuable. Every time we sit in a chair we do not have to reconstruct the experiences by which we learned that chairs will bear our weight; we presuppose that chairs will support our weight. We rightly presuppose when we read in the Bible that God is good, and thus we appropriately ask why he allows suffering. Imagine a situation where we did not even ask this question! Our presuppositions can provoke us to ask profound and crucial questions.

On the other hand, our presuppositions can blind us to the truth as well. For example, we may assume that James 5:13–18 cannot possibly refer to physical healing and instead it describes spiritual weakness because physical healing does not occur today. Yet such a presupposition or preunderstanding may blind us to what the text is actually saying.

The crucial question is this: Can we detect in ourselves incorrect presuppositions and modify our worldview so that we can understand what Paul (or any author) intended when he wrote his letters? If this is not possible, then it follows that no learning or change in thinking is possible for human beings. We are trapped in our own culture and worldview. And if we can never break out of our own preunderstanding, why should we ever attempt to comprehend another person's point of view? We could never really understand another anyway. Such a nihilistic view should be rejected, for it contradicts human experience. We have understood and can understand those whose thinking is alien to us, even though such a process may take great effort. If we are willing to let the Scriptures challenge our most cherished ideas and opinions, then we will be able to understand the Scriptures and let them change our minds.

10. See G. N. Stanton, "Presuppositions in New Testament Criticism," in *New Testament Interpretation: Essays on Principles and Methods*, ed. I. H. Marshall (Grand Rapids: Eerdmans, 1977), 60–71; R. Bultmann, "Is Exegesis Without Presuppositions Possible?" in *Existence and Faith* (London: Hodder & Stoughton, 1960), 289–96.

The Art of Interpretation

This book will focus on the methodology that should be used in interpreting the Pauline letters. Methodology focuses upon the science of interpretation, that is, the principles and procedures that are essential for exegesis. Nevertheless, interpretation is also an artistic enterprise. For instance, the forming of an hypothesis regarding the interpretation of a passage is a product of the imagination. Since exegesis is both a science and an art, we cannot expect that the right interpretation will automatically emerge by following the steps outlined in this book. In every interpretation we are dealing with degrees of probability in formulating an interpretation. Absolute certainty is not possible. This does not lead to relativism in interpretation, for some interpretations are more probable than others. Evidence and logic are used to establish the probability of various interpretations. The interpretation that is the most coherent and comprehensive is the most probable. Even scientists recognize today that nothing can be proved absolutely. Nevertheless, some things are more probable than others. For example, it is possible that the world we live in is an illusion and life is a dream, but such a view of reality is not the most probable. So too, the interpretations of some biblical texts are virtually certain, while in other texts the meaning is more debatable. The careful interpreter acknowledges a sliding scale of probability and emphasizes the truth of an interpretation accordingly.

1

Understanding the Nature of Letters

The Question of Genre

Perhaps the most important issue in interpretation is the issue of genre. If we misunderstand the genre of a text, the rest of our analysis will be askew. If we interpret a fairy tale as a historical report, the interpretation may be profound and insightful in many ways, but the interpretation will be fatally flawed from the beginning because of a misreading of the genre of the text.

All of the thirteen writings attributed to Paul are letters. The most unsophisticated reader intuitively grasps that letters are quite different from Gospels or other books like Acts and Revelation. The question for the interpreter is: What difference does it make that Paul wrote letters rather than Gospels? Or, to put it another way: What can we learn about the genre of the Pauline letters that will help us interpret them more accurately? This chapter will attempt to answer this question.

Letters or Epistles?

It is important to discern the nature of the Pauline letters before interpreting them, and in contemporary scholarship the relationship between Pauline letters and other letters that were written in the ancient Greco-Roman world is being keenly studied.[1] Adolf Deissmann argued in the early part of this century that Paul's writings should be designated as *letters* in distinction from *epistles*.[2] Epistles, he maintained, were artistically written for a wider public and intended for posterity, while letters were dashed off to address specific situations and problems and were never intended to be literary compositions. Paul's letters, he claimed, are not literary treatises. They are occasional documents (i.e., written to specific situations) written in the language of the common people. According to Deissmann, Paul wrote his letters to react to specific problems that occurred in the churches but Paul never conceived of them as documents that would continue to function authoritatively in the future life of the church.

Deissmann was surely right in stressing that Paul wrote his letters to specific situations and to address particular problems in his congregations. There is no indication that Paul expected subsequent generations to read them. Nevertheless, Deissmann's neat distinction between letters and epistles has been rightly questioned by contemporary scholarship, and his thesis should be modified for the following reasons. First, Deissmann overemphasized the similarity between the papyri and the Pauline letters. Even a cursory reading of the papyri and the Pauline letters demonstrates the remarkable differences that exist between the two bodies of literature. For instance, Paul's letters display a literary quality and structure that are not evident in the papyri. In fact, some recent scholars have contended that the Pauline letters are patterned after Greek rhetoric. Even if these scholars have overemphasized this point, they are surely right in asserting that the letters are literary products. Paul's letters are occasional in nature, and yet they show every evidence of being carefully written compositions.

Second, Deissmann rightly stressed the occasional nature of the Pauline letters (a topic we will address below), but the

1. The literature on this topic is immense. The following are especially helpful: W. G. Doty, *Letters in Primitive Christianity* (Philadelphia: Fortress, 1973); S. K. Stowers, *Letter Writing in Greco-Roman Antiquity* (Philadelphia: Westminster, 1986); J. L. White, *Light from Ancient Letters* (Philadelphia: Fortress, 1986); D. E. Aune, *The New Testament in Its Literary Environment* (Philadelphia: Westminster, 1987).

2. *Light from the Ancient East: The New Testament Illustrated by Recently Discovered Texts of the Graeco-Roman World* (London: Hodder & Stoughton, 1927), 228–41.

letters were not merely private individual letters. Paul wrote them as an apostle, and he expected them to be read in and obeyed by the Christian community (1 Cor. 14:37; 1 Thess. 5:27; 2 Thess. 3:14). Indeed, even though Colossians addressed a specific situation, Paul thought its message would be helpful to the Laodiceans (Col. 4:16). Apparently Paul believed that his specific and occasional instructions for the Colossians had a wider significance so that his words were relevant not only for the Colossians but also for the Laodiceans. Furthermore, at times Paul clearly said that his words were in fact the very word of God (1 Cor. 14:37–38; see Gal. 1:8). He did not conceive of his letters as mere human advice (see 1 Thess. 2:13). Thus, the letters had a normative and authoritative status from the beginning (which is perhaps why they were preserved), and letters written to particular communities could apply to other churches as well.

Structure of Pauline Letters

An analysis of the structure of Pauline letters is essential for proper interpretation. The most helpful tool for an analysis of forms in Paul is the book titled *Pauline Parallels*.[3] Here Pauline passages which reflect the same literary form or are on the same topic are collected together so that the reader can compare and contrast parallel passages. Paul's letters follow the format of most Greco-Roman letters of his day, containing an *opening*, the *body*, and the *closing*.

The Opening

The opening usually has the following four elements: (1) the sender of the letter is named (e.g., "Paul"); (2) the addressees of the letter are specified (e.g., "to the Thessalonians"); (3) the salutation ("grace and peace"); and (4) the prayer which was usually a thanksgiving ("I thank God").

Sender of Letter

Paul adds his own twist to each of these conventional patterns in the opening of the letters. He often designates himself

3. F. O. Francis and J. P. Sampley, eds., *Pauline Parallels*, 2d ed. (Philadelphia: Fortress, 1984).

as an "apostle" or as a "servant" when he names himself as
the sender. Also Paul typically lists various cosenders in his
letters: "Paul and Silas and Timothy" (1 Thess. 1:1; 2 Thess.
1:1); "Paul and Timothy" (Phil. 1:1); "Paul . . . and all the
brethren with me" (Gal. 1:1–2); "Paul and Sosthenes" (1 Cor.
1:1). Not all the letters, however, have cosenders (Rom. 1:1;
Eph. 1:1; 1 Tim. 1:1; 2 Tim. 1:1; Tit. 1:1). Paul may name
some of these cosenders because they participated with him
in the planting of the church. I think it is doubtful that the
cosenders played a major role in the actual composition of
the letters. By referring to his partners Paul may also be indicating that the gospel he preaches and writes about is not his
private preserve; the brethren with him recognize its authority as well. For example, the inclusion of "all the brethren with
me" in Galatians 1:2 is an indication that Paul's gospel is
accepted as truth by the Christian community from which he
writes. It is the Galatians, not Paul, who have deviated from
the apostolic traditions.

How Paul designates himself is significant interpretively.
His authority as an apostle is highlighted and expanded upon
in Galatians (1:1) where his gospel is being questioned, and
the Galatians have wandered from the truth. In Romans 1:1–7
Paul elaborates upon his apostleship and his gospel in order
to introduce himself to his readers in Rome; Paul previews
the letter in the opening, for the rest of the letter unfolds his
gospel for Jews and Gentiles. On the other hand, omission of
any reference to his apostolic authority in 1 Thessalonians is
perhaps one clue that there was no dispute regarding Paul's
apostolic authority in Thessalonica. So too in the personal
and warm letter to Philemon Paul identifies himself as
δέσμιος Χριστοῦ Ἰησοῦ ("prisoner of Christ Jesus," Philem. 1).
In writing to a personal friend in a delicate situation Paul
does not want to appeal to his apostolic authority. Moreover,
his self-designation fits with the emphasis on his present status and Onesimus' usefulness to him in prison (Philem. 9–13).

In the letter to the Philippians, which contains several suggestions that the church is plagued with lack of unity (Phil.
1:27–2:4; 4:2–3), Paul does not call himself an apostle, but
designates himself and Timothy as δοῦλοι ("slaves," 1:1).
From the very beginning Paul is using himself as a model and
example for the Philippians. Disunity is caused by self-exalta-

tion and the failure to be a servant to brothers and sisters.
Paul, Timothy (2:19–24), Epaphroditus (2:25–30), and most
significantly Messiah Jesus (2:5–11) all have the mind-set of a
servant.

Addressees

The addressees in Paul's letters are Christian communities,
and Paul has these communities in view even when he writes
to individuals such as Philemon, Timothy, and Titus. Paul
adds distinctive features here as well. The Thessalonians are
addressed as those who are "in God the Father and the Lord
Jesus Christ" (1 Thess. 1:1; see 2 Thess. 1:1, which in Greek
is precisely the same with the addition of the pronoun ἡμῶν).
He often calls his readers "saints," "beloved," "called," or
"sanctified." In Philippians Paul specifically mentions the
"overseers and deacons" (Phil. 1:1). Nowhere else does he
mention church leaders in the addressee section, and so the
interpreter must probe to discover the reason for this distinctive feature in Philippians. The church of Corinth was rent by
division (1 Cor. 1:10–4:21), and so Paul's inclusion of "all
those who call upon the name of our Lord Jesus Christ in
every place, both theirs and ours" (1 Cor. 1:2) is intended to
remind the Corinthians of the wider scope of the body of
Christ. This foreshadows Paul's emphasis on the traditions of
other churches in 1 Corinthians (1 Cor. 11:2, 16, 23–26; 14:33b;
15:1ff.). The same emphasis on the wider scope of God's
church also appears in 2 Corinthians 1:1.

Greeting

The typical Hellenistic greeting in letters was χαίρειν
("greetings"; see Acts 15:23). Paul, however, christianizes the
greeting by changing it to the Greek word χάρις ("grace"), a
distinctive element in his gospel. Most Hebrew or Aramaic
letters would greet the recipients with the word שָׁלוֹם ("peace"),
and this may account for Paul's inclusion of the word εἰρήνη
("peace") in the greeting. Perhaps both "grace and peace"
were included because Paul wanted to include both
Hellenistic and Jewish literary conventions in his greetings to
represent his gospel's emphasis on the equal standing of
Gentiles and Jews before God (Gal. 3:28–29; Rom. 1:16;
15:7–13). Paul adds the word ἔλεος ("mercy"), which is also
found in some Semitic letters, to his greeting in 1 Timothy
1:1 and 2 Timothy 1:2.

Almost all of the greetings in Paul's letters are from "God the Father and the Lord Jesus Christ." The exceptions are Colossians 1:2, where only God the Father is mentioned, and 1 Thessalonians 1:1, where Paul simply greets the readers with the words "grace and peace to you." In Titus 1:4 Paul adds the attribution "our Savior" to "Christ Jesus," probably because savior is a central theme in this letter. In Galatians 1:4 Paul adds a statement on the purpose of the giving of God's Son, namely, "[he] gave himself for our sins to rescue us from the present evil age." Here he signals one of the major themes of the letter. The Galatians have been bewitched and have failed to see the significance of the cross of Christ (see 2:21; 3:1, 13; 4:4–5; 5:11; 6:12, 14). If they capitulate to the false gospel, then they will be entrapped in the present evil age from which Christ died to liberate them. Careful reading of the opening is essential because it alerts the reader to central themes that will be developed in the letter.

Prayer

The last element of the opening is the prayer.[4] Hellenistic letters usually contained a health wish and then a prayer to the gods for the addressee. Almost all of Paul's letters have a thanksgiving (e.g., 1 Cor. 1:4–9; Col. 1:3–8) or a blessing (2 Cor. 1:3–7; Eph. 1:3–14).[5] Only Galatians and Titus lack a thanksgiving; the latter lacks it because Paul was writing a brief letter of instruction to his trusted assistant, while the former lacks it because the abandonment of the gospel by the Galatians rather than thanksgiving was in the forefront of Paul's mind. He does not follow any set pattern in his thanksgivings. The thanksgiving in 1 Corinthians 1:4–9 is discrete and easily separable. In Philippians 1:3–11 and Colossians 1:3–14 a petition is added to the thanksgiving section. On the other hand, in 1 Thessalonians the thanksgiving period is longer (1:2–3:13) and is punctuated with other themes. The interpreter should be careful to allow each one of the letters to express its distinctive message, since Paul's style does not necessarily follow any particular pattern.

4. For a study of this section of the letters, three books are particularly significant: P. Schubert, *Form and Function of Pauline Thanksgivings* (Berlin: Töpelmann, 1939); P. T. O'Brien, *Introductory Thanksgivings in the Letters of Paul* (Leiden: Brill, 1977); G. P. Wiles, *Paul's Intercessory Prayers: The Significance of the Intercessory Prayer Passages in the Letters of St. Paul* (London: Cambridge University Press, 1974).

5. The thanksgiving section follows in Ephesians 1:15ff.

One of the most important conclusions that has been established by the work of Schubert, O'Brien, and Wiles is the function of the prayers in the Pauline argument. Paul's thanksgivings and intercessory prayers often signal the major themes in the letter, and thus demand careful analysis. The thanksgiving sections reveal Paul's pastoral care for the Christian communities and secure their good will. They also have a didactic and parenetic purpose, instructing and exhorting the readers in the Christian life. Finally, a liturgical element is probably present as well, making the public reading of the letter appropriate for corporate worship.

An example may help here. In 1 Corinthians 1:4–9 Paul thanks God for the spiritual gifts and the richness of knowledge in the Corinthian community. We know from the rest of the letter (chaps. 1–4; 8–10; 12–14) that the Corinthians misunderstood the role of knowledge and spiritual gifts. They wrongly exalted themselves for their superior knowledge and their experience of spiritual gifts. Paul acknowledges from the beginning of the letter that spiritual gifts and knowledge are to be celebrated. Nevertheless, the thanksgiving section stresses that all praise should go to *God* for these benefits, not to the Corinthians. There is no justification for pride or self–exaltation. The thanksgiving anticipates, then, Paul's subsequent response to the problems in the Corinthian community.

The Closing

It is often difficult to determine precisely where the body of a Pauline letter ends and where its closing begins. Many of Paul's letters include the following elements in the closing.

1. Travel plans or personal situation (Rom. 15:22–29; 1 Cor. 16:5–9; Eph. 6:21–22; Col. 4:7–9; 2 Tim. 4:9–17; Tit. 3:12);
2. Prayer (Rom. 15:33; 16:25–27; 1 Thess. 5:23; 2 Thess. 3:16);
3. Commendation of fellow workers (Rom. 16:1–2; 1 Cor. 16:10–12);
4. Prayer requests (Rom. 15:30–32; Col. 4:2–4; Eph. 6:18–20; 1 Thess. 5:25);

5. Greetings (Rom. 16:3–16, 21–23; 1 Cor. 16:19–21; 2 Cor. 13:12; Phil. 4:21–22; Col. 4:10–15; 2 Tim. 4:19–21; Tit. 3:15a; Philem. 23–24);
6. Final instructions and exhortations (Rom. 16:17–20a; 1 Cor. 16:13–18; 2 Cor. 13:11; Gal. 6:11–17; Col. 4:16–18a; 1 Thess. 5:27; 2 Thess. 3:14–15; 1 Tim. 6:20–21a; Philem. 21–22);
7. Holy kiss (1 Cor. 16:20b; 2 Cor. 13:12a; 1 Thess. 5:26);
8. Autographed greeting (1 Cor. 16:21; Gal. 6:11; Col. 4:18a; 2 Thess. 3:17; Philem. 19);
9. A χάρις benediction (Rom. 16:20b; 1 Cor. 16:23–24; 2 Cor. 13:13; Gal. 6:18; Eph. 6:24; Phil. 4:23; Col. 4:18b; 1 Thess. 5:28; 2 Thess. 3:18; 1 Tim. 6:21b; 2 Tim. 4:22b; Tit. 3:15b; Philem. 25).

The order of these items varies in the different letters, lacking any obvious preformed pattern. The only constant is that the benediction comes at the end, except in Romans. Most Hellenistic letters of the day ended with the word "farewell" Ἔρρωσθε or Ἔρρωσο (see Acts 15:29). Once again we see Paul's christianization of a typical formula.

We should emphasize that Paul exercises great freedom in the closing, depending on the letter he is writing. Thus, apart from the final exhortation in Galatians 6:11–17, the closing is remarkably brief in Galatians (6:18), but very long in Romans (Rom. 16:1–27), punctuated with one exhortation (16:17–20) and a unique prayer and doxology (16:25–27).[6] The unusual nature of the conclusion leads the interpreter to ponder the significance of such a closing in this letter. 1 Corinthians closes with an exhortation to submit to the house of Stephanas and other leaders (1 Cor. 16:15–18), while in Colossians the church is charged to swap letters with the Laodiceans and a special charge is delivered to Archippus (Col. 4:16–17). Once again we see that Paul is not bound to any preexisting formula, and the interpreter would do well to scout out any unusual features and try to explain their inclusion.

The Body

The next major section of Pauline letters, the body, is becoming the subject of intensive investigation for literary

---

6. The last passage is textually disputed, but probably belongs at the end of Romans. See the brief discussion of this text in the next chapter on textual criticism.

patterns and structure. Scholars have not reached a consensus yet on the structure of Pauline letters, and this is hardly surprising since the letters exhibit remarkable diversity. The wise interpreter will begin with a careful analysis of the contents of the letter itself instead of trying to fit it into any pre-existing type.

Introductory Formulas

Scholars have noted that the body of Paul's letters often begin with certain formulaic phrases.[7] The following types, among others, have been identified:

1. Disclosure formulas: "I do not want you to be ignorant" (Rom. 1:13); "For we do not want you to be ignorant" (2 Cor. 1:8); "Now I want you to know, brothers" (Phil. 1:12); "For you yourselves know brethren" (1 Thess. 2:1);
2. Request formulas: "Now I exhort (παρακαλέω) you" (1 Cor. 1:10); "Now we ask (ἐρωτῶμεν) you brethren" (2 Thess. 2:1);
3. Expression of Astonishment: "I am amazed that you are so quickly departing" (Gal. 1:6). (I think, however, that the expression of astonishment is hardly a typical literary technique, but was called forth by the situation that Paul addressed at Galatia.)

We should reiterate here that the letters do not all follow the same pattern, and some lack a discernible transition from the opening to the body (e.g., Colossians). In some of the examples given above, for example, the beginning point of the body of the letter is debatable. So again, the best advice for the interpreter is to read the letter on its own terms. Follow carefully the argument of the letter itself, noting literary patterns as they occur.

Rhetorical Criticism

Some scholars using the tool of rhetorical criticism in the study of the Pauline letters have investigated the body of

7. J. L. White, "Introductory Formulae in the Body of the Pauline Letter," *Journal of Biblical Literature* 90 (1971): 91–97.

some Pauline letters in more detail.[8] "Rhetorical criticism attempts to understand the effect that conventional forms of argumentation and structure used in the Greco-Roman world had on early Christian literary composition."[9] Three types of rhetoric were employed in the Greco-Roman world: (1) judicial, (2) deliberative, and (3) epideictic. Judicial rhetoric was the language of the law court and was used to convince an audience about the rightness or wrongness of past actions. Accusation or defense were the two forms of argumentation that were typically used. A speaker used deliberative rhetoric to convince an audience about the future. What action should be taken in the future and why? Persuasion and dissuasion were the two forms of argumentation employed. Epideictic rhetoric was not persuasive in nature as were the former two types. The goal of epideictic rhetoric was to celebrate common values and ideals.

Greco-Roman rhetorical theory has been specifically applied to the Pauline letters. A number of suggestions regarding the classification of particular letters has been made, although we can note only a few of them here. For example, Galatians has been identified as an apologetic or deliberative letter,[10] while 1 Thessalonians, 1 Corinthians, and Philippians have been identified as parenetic letters, that is, letters in which Paul exhorted Christian communities.[11] Second Corinthians has been described as a letter of apologetic self-commendation in which Paul commended his apostolic ministry,[12] and Philemon has been seen as a letter of recommendation for

8. For a helpful introduction to Greek rhetoric, see G. A. Kennedy, *New Testament Interpretation through Rhetorical Criticism* (Chapel Hill: University of North Carolina, 1984). Aune also has an invaluable and concise discussion in his *Literary Environment*, 198–99.

9. Aune, *Literary Environment*, 198.

10. See further discussion on this below.

11. Aune (*Literary Environment*, 203, 206, 210–11) described 1 Corinthians as a letter of parenesis and advice, Philippians as one of gratitude and parenesis, and 1 Thessalonians as parenetic. For an analysis of 1–2 Thessalonians in particular, see R. Jewett, *The Thessalonian Correspondence: Pauline Rhetoric and Millenarian Piety* (Philadelphia: Fortress, 1986), 63–87. Jewett understood 1 Thessalonians as an epideictic letter and 2 Thessalonians as deliberative. His analysis is questionable on a number of points, especially the claim that 1 Thessalonians 4:1–5:22 is the *probatio* of the letter.

12. L. L. Belleville, "A Letter of Apologetic Self-Commendation: 2 Cor. 1:8–7:16," *Novum Testamentum* 31 (1989): 142–63. Although Belleville limited her study to the first seven chapters, the whole of 2 Corinthians (if one subscribes to the unity of the letter) can be designated as a letter of apologetic self-commendation. Second Corinthians 12:19 shows that Paul expected the Corinthians to understand the letter in these terms. See F. Young and D. F. Young (*Meaning and Truth in 2 Corinthians* [Grand Rapids: Eerdmans, 1987], 36–44) who understood the whole of 2 Corinthians to be an apologetic letter.

Onesimus or as a deliberative letter in which Paul attempted to persuade Philemon.[13]

The most notable example of rhetorical criticism is H. D. Betz's analysis of Galatians.[14] A short discussion of Betz's proposal will help us to understand more concretely the relation of rhetorical criticism to Pauline literature. Betz saw the letter as a judicial apologetic letter. The argument of the letter presupposes a court of law. The defendant is Paul, the plaintiff is identified as Paul's opponents, and the jury is the Galatians themselves. The letter as a whole should be understood as Paul's self-apology.

Betz saw the structure of the letter as follows:

Prescript 1:1–5

Body 1:6–6:10

Exordium 1:6–11 (reason for the letter)

Narratio 1:12–2:14 (narration of events to make denial of Paul's guilt plausible)

Propositio 2:15–21 (sums up the previous section and is the transition to the next section; main thesis of letter)

Probatio 3:1–4:31 (argument designed to *prove* Paul's defense)

Paraenesis 5:1–6:10 (exhortation)

Postscript 6:11–18 (contains the *peroratio* or *conclusio;* the former is the last reminder by the author, and the latter is written to make a strong emotional impression on the readers; this section summarizes the major issues in the letter).

Betz's work is very impressive, and anyone who has read Galatians can see the points of contact between Galatians and the rhetorical pattern identified by Betz. By focusing on the structure of the letter, he proved that the letter was carefully

13. For the former, see Aune, *Literary Environment,* 211–21, and for the latter, F. F. Church, "Rhetorical Structure and Design in Paul's Letter to Philemon," *Harvard Theological Review* 71 (1978): 17–33.

14. See his article, "Literary Composition and Function of Paul's Letter to the Galatians," *New Testament Studies* 21 (1975): 353–79. In his commentary on Galatians (*A Commentary on Paul's Letter to the Churches in Galatia* [Philadelphia: Fortress, 1979]), he applied his analysis in more depth; see esp. pp. 14–25 for his layout and explanation of the structure of the letter.

written and structured and that Paul was probably influenced by the rhetorical conventions employed by others in his day.

Despite the valuable and provocative features of Betz's analysis, it has several weaknesses which suggest that the letter is not really an apologetic letter:[15] (1) the parenetical section does not fit into the rhetorical structure of apologetic letters, as even Betz admitted; (2) the exordium in Greek rhetoric was designed to secure the good will of the audience, but Paul's harsh words in Galatians 1:6–11 would hardly endear him to the Galatians; (3) Betz built his model on the literary *theory* of the apologetic letter, but he did not provide a single example of an actual apologetic letter for comparison with Galatians; and (4) the emphasis on Greco-Roman rhetoric wrongly downplays the fact that Paul was a Jew who employed exegetical practices typically used in the synagogues.

R. G. Hall suggested that Galatians is better understood as a deliberative letter.[16] The letter is not primarily judicial (i.e., a defense against opponents), but persuasive: Paul wanted the Galatians to embrace him and his gospel and to repudiate the opponents and their gospel. Hall was certainly correct that Paul's primary purpose was to persuade the Galatians, and thus it is appropriate to designate Galatians as a deliberative letter. Nevertheless, the generic classification proposed by Hall, although valuable, should not be overrated. Hall's analysis of Galatians was so general—it lacked the specificity of Betz's analysis—that the identification of the letter within the categories of a particular genre does not contribute a great deal to one's specific understanding of Galatians. To put it another way, most readers are aware that Galatians is a persuasive letter even if they are unaware of Greek rhetoric.

Some writers have tried to unfold the rhetorical pattern of Paul's letters in more detail. Such detailed analyses, as we have seen in the case of Betz, often fail because they impose

15. For these criticisms see the following: W. D. Davies, P. W. Meyer, and D. E. Aune, "Review: *Galatians: A Commentary on Paul's Letter to the Churches of Galatia* by Hans Dieter Betz," *Religious Studies Review* 7 (1981): 310–28; G. Lyons, *Pauline Autobiography: Toward a New Understanding* (Atlanta: Scholars, 1985), 112–19. Of course, not all of these scholars think the same criticisms are relevant.

16. R. G. Hall, "The Rhetorical Outline for Galatians: A Reconsideration," *Journal of Biblical Literature* 106 (1987): 277–87; see also Lyons, *Pauline Autobiography*, 112–19, 173–75; Aune, *Literary Environment*, 206–08.

the structure of Greek rhetoric upon the Pauline letters. For instance, Smit excluded the parenetical section of Galatians (5:13–6:10) in order to sustain his rhetorical schema.[17] Such a desperate expedient is really an indication that the rhetorical schema proposed is a failure. Indeed, one of the weaknesses of the rhetorical approach seems to be that the more detailed the analysis of the letter is, the less convincing the proposed rhetorical structure appears.

On the other hand, identifying the genre of particular letters has value. Many of Paul's letters are appropriately described as parenetic, and 2 Corinthians has many similarities with apologetic letters of self-commendation. Such generic classifications help the reader to see the overall purpose of the letter, although the reader must beware of pigeonholing Paul's letters too neatly, since the more specific one becomes in identifying the genre of a letter, the greater the danger that specific elements of the letter that do not fit the classification are suppressed or forced to fit the pattern. Thus, to describe the basic genre of a particular letter does not absolve the reader of the responsibility of tracing Paul's argument carefully in each letter, discerning the unique structure of each writing by a careful examination of the text. Moreover, the interpreter should not forget that Paul was a Jewish writer who employed Jewish exegetical practices. This should protect the interpreter from overemphasizing Paul's dependence upon Greek rhetorical schemas.

What can we conclude concerning the application of rhetorical criticism to Pauline letters? Rhetorical criticism has made a positive contribution to Pauline studies in three respects. First, Paul probably had a general knowledge of the rhetorical patterns of his day since he lived within Greco-Roman culture. Second, even if Paul had no knowledge at all of Greek rhetoric (which is unlikely), Greek rhetoric classified and described the elements of good argumentation. Since Paul was a careful thinker, it is not surprising that his letters evince some parallels with Greek rhetoric. Paul was by nature and education an effective advocate, and Greek rhetoric aptly describes the elements of such effective advocacy. Even today

17. J. Smit, "The Letter of Paul to the Galatians: A Deliberative Speech," *New Testament Studies* 35 (1989): 1–26. Smit maintained that Galatians 5:13–6:10 was written later and inserted into the letter by Paul, but such a later insertion lacks evidence; Smit seems to have suggested it in order to sustain his rhetorical theory.

effective debaters use many of the elements of Greek rhetoric whether or not they are conscious of it. Third, rhetorical criticism is valuable because it takes Paul's letters seriously as literary creations and as argumentative tracts. This last point is the most crucial. It is tempting to focus exclusively on reconstructing the history behind Paul's letters instead of analyzing the argument of the letter itself. Rhetorical criticism rightly directs the reader to a close analysis of the structure and argumentation contained in the Pauline epistles.

Some Specific Forms in Paul's Letters

Rhetorical criticism examines the structure of Pauline letters as a whole, but the interpreter should also be aware of specific formal features in the Pauline letters.

The Diatribe

For some time scholars have agreed that Paul used a diatribe style in his letters. In a recent work Stowers argued that the diatribe had its origin in the classroom where teachers used it to provoke learning.[18] The characteristic feature of the diatribe is its conversational nature. The teacher (or writer) anticipates a possible objection or response to his argument, and puts the question or objection in the student's words and responds to it.

Several examples from Romans will illustrate Paul's use of the diatribe. In Romans 2:25–29 Paul said that the uncircumcised Gentile who observes the law is spiritually circumcised and a spiritual Jew. Paul anticipated an objection in the following verse: "What advantage, then, is there in being a Jew, or what value is there in circumcision?" (Rom. 3:1 NIV). A similar feature appears in Romans 6:1. In Romans 5:20 Paul said that grace abounds even more where sin has increased. Then in 6:1 he voiced the possible objection: "What shall we say, then? Shall we go on sinning so that grace may increase?" Sometimes Paul addressed the opponent with a direct statement: "But who are you, O man, to talk back to God?" (Rom. 9:20); and "Or do you show contempt for the riches of his

---

18. S. K. Stowers, *The Diatribe and Paul's Letter to the Romans* (Chico: Scholars, 1981). The older view was that the diatribe originated in the preaching of Cynics and Stoics. See R. Bultmann, *Der Stil der paulinischen Predigt und die kynisch-stoische Diatribe* (Göttingen: Vandenhoeck & Ruprecht, 1910).

kindness, tolerance and patience . . . ?" (Rom. 2:4). Paul often rejected the conclusion of the objector with the words μὴ γένοιτο, that is, "By no means!"(Rom. 3:4; 6:2, 15; 7:7, 13; 9:14; 11:1).

The dialogical method is an effective teaching device. Paul placed objections and false conclusions at key places in the argument, and then repudiated them. If Stowers is correct that the diatribe is a teaching device that emanates from the classroom and philosophical schools, then it follows that the objector with whom Paul debated in Romans is not necessarily a real opponent in Rome. If this is the case, then the letter to the Romans was not necessarily written to address specific problems in Rome. The problem with Stower's thesis, however, is that we cannot demonstrate that Paul borrowed the diatribal style from the philosophical schools, nor are Paul's letters similar to philosophical discussions in the classroom. Even if he did borrow the diatribe from the philosophical schools, we cannot prove that he used the diatribe in the same way the schools did. Paul had a creative mind, and so he could have borrowed a rhetorical technique and modified it in addressing his readers. Moreover, perhaps Paul's Pharisaic training exposed him to the diatribe style of argument, or perhaps the natural development of Paul's fertile mind led to it. Paul's missionary work in the East had prepared him for possible objections to his gospel, and this may account for the appearance of objections in Romans. In short, Paul clearly used a diatribal style, but we cannot establish that he used this device as it was used in the philosophical schools.

Parenesis

The Pauline letters are awash in parenesis (i.e., exhortations). Indeed, some of the letters are best described as parenetic letters. For example, the whole of 1 Thessalonians can be classified as parenetic. In Romans the parenetical section (12:1–15:13) appears to be neatly separated from the earlier part of the letter. Parenesis should be considered, however, as an integral part of Paul's purpose in writing Romans, and exhortations are present in the earlier part of the letter as well (see Rom. 6). Aune helpfully distinguished between letters that have a *parenetic* style, where the entire letter is marked by exhortations (such as 1 Thessalonians), and *epistolary*

parenesis, which is found in the concluding sections of some
letters.[19] For instance, Philippians, 1 Thessalonians, and
Colossians have a parenetic style. On the other hand, epistolary parenesis is found at the end of Romans (12:1–15:13),
Galatians (5:13–6:10), Ephesians (4:1–6:20), and Colossians
(3:1–4:6). A letter (e.g., Colossians) can possibly have both of
these features at the same time, that is, a parenetic style and a
concluding section of epistolary parenesis.

Pauline parenesis cannot be squeezed into any single mold.
Paul clearly directed some of his exhortations to the specific
situation that his readers faced. This is clearly the case in
Colossians 2 and in much of 1 Corinthians. On the other
hand, Paul may also have warned his readers of *potential*
problems rather than *actual* problems. We err if we assume
that when Paul gave parenetical advice to a congregation, the
congregation was failing in that area. For example, Paul's
warning on sexual purity in 1 Thessalonians 4:3–8 does not
necessarily mean that the Thessalonians were having a great
problem with sexual immorality. We shall return to this topic
again when we discuss the issue of mirror reading.

As we said above, some parenesis is clearly directed to a
specific situation. Other parenesis seems to be more conventional, and could be applied to almost any situation.[20] The
household tables, in which Paul exhorted wives, husbands,
children, slaves, and masters (Eph. 5:22–6:9; Col. 3:18–4:1),
reflect general moral advice that Paul could have given to all
Christian communities. However, we have no indication that
this material was included in Colossians or Ephesians
because these churches had problems with these issues.[21]

Similarly, Paul included many vice and virtue lists in his

19. Aune, *Literary Environment*, 191.
20. This distinction within parenesis is supported by P. Vielhauer, *Geschichte der urchristlichen Literatur*, 2d ed. (Berlin: Walter de Gruyter, 1978), 50.
21. J. E. Crouch thought that the household code was intended to restrain women and slaves whose understanding of Galatians 3:28 precipitated social unrest (*The Origin and Intention of the Colossian Haustafel* [Göttingen: Vandenhoeck & Ruprecht, 1972], 120–145). D. E. Balch said that the household code in 1 Peter has an apologetic function (*Let Wives Be Submissive: The Domestic Code in 1 Peter* [Chico: Scholars, 1981], 81–109). The view of Balch is possible from 1 Peter, although there is no evidence that the house-hold tables have this function in Colossians or Ephesians. Crouch's view regarding the function of Galatians 3:28 cannot be substantiated from the exegesis of Colossians or Ephesians. For a brief summary of scholarship on household tables, see R. P. Martin, "Haustafeln," in *The New International Dictionary of New Testament Theology*, ed. C. Brown, 4 vols. (Grand Rapids: Zondervan, 1975–86), 3:928–32.

letters (Rom. 1:29–31; 1 Cor. 5:10–11; 6:9–11; Gal. 5:19–23; Eph. 4:19, 25–32; 5:3–5; Col. 3:5–9, 12–15; etc.). Surely these lists reflect typical human problems, but the inclusion of a vice list or an exhortation to particular virtues does not necessarily indicate that the community was experiencing a problem in the areas cited.[22] Other evidence from the letter is necessary to show that items in a vice or virtue list were mentioned because of a specific problem in the church.

Hymns and Confessional Statements

The presence of hymns and traditional material in Paul is the subject of continuing investigation today.[23] Hymns (Eph. 5:14; Phil. 2:6–11; Col. 1:15–20; 1 Tim. 3:16) and traditional materials (Rom. 1:3–4; 3:24–26; 4:25; 10:9; Gal. 1:4) are identified in many different places in the Pauline corpus. The above examples are only a few of the numerous passages that are so designated. Without a doubt Paul used traditional material, as 1 Corinthians 11:23–26 and 15:1ff. demonstrate.

Much of the discussion on hymns and traditional materials in Paul is intended to excavate the pre-Pauline history of the church. Interpreters reconstruct the theology, or part of the theology, of the early church by delineating the pre-Pauline form of the traditional materials. This arena of study is provocative and helpful (although the interpreter should be on guard against unwarranted speculation), for it may provide access to the history of pre-Pauline Christianity. Nevertheless, the interpreter of Paul's letters does not have as a primary goal the meaning of the pre-Pauline form of the material. What we are interested in is the meaning of the final redaction of the hymn or creedal formula as it presently exists in canonical form.

When Paul used traditional materials, he presumably

22. For two English articles on vice and virtue lists, see B. S. Easton, "New Testament Ethical Lists," *Journal of Biblical Literature* 51 (1932): 1–12, and N. J. McEleney, "The Vice Lists of the Pastoral Epistles," *Catholic Biblical Quarterly* 36 (1974): 203–19.

23. See, e.g., V. H. Neufeld, *The Earliest Christian Confessions* (Grand Rapids: Eerdmans, 1963), esp. pp. 42–68; J. H. Charlesworth, "A Prolegomenon to a New Study of the Jewish Background of the Hymns and Prayers in the New Testament," *Journal of Jewish Studies* 33 (1982): 265–85; R. P. Martin, *Carmen Christi: Philippians 2:5–11 in Recent Interpretation and in the Setting of Early Christian Worship* (Grand Rapids: Eerdmans, 1983); J. T. Sanders, *The New Testament Christological Hymns: Their Historical Religious Background* (Cambridge: Cambridge University Press, 1971).

adapted them for his own purposes and integrated them into the flow of thought of his letters. One should not base an interpretation on the alleged pre-Pauline form of a hymn, or on a theory that attempts to establish the Pauline additions to the original hymn. Such an enterprise is often too speculative,[24] and one can end up arguing in a vicious circle. We may not know how a hymn or creedal formula was interpreted by the pre-Pauline community, but we can know Paul's meaning as he expressed it in the text.

Colossians 1:15–20 may illustrate why this enterprise of attempting to detect the pre-Pauline form of a hymn is not productive. Scholars cannot agree on whether this hymn derives from Gnosticism, rabbinic Judaism, or Hellenistic Judaism.[25] For example, Schweizer, who saw the hymn as originating in Hellenistic Judaism, thought that four elements were added to the hymn by the author of Colossians: (1) "whether thrones or dominions or rulers or authorities" (v. 16); (2) "the church" (v. 18); (3) "so that he himself might come to have first place in everything" (v. 18); and (4) "the blood of the cross" (v. 19).[26] In focusing upon one of the alleged additions to the hymn, namely, the word "church," we can begin to comprehend how Schweizer understood the pre-Pauline theology of the hymn. The original hymn did not speak of Christ as being "head of the church"; rather, it said

24. M. D. Hooker may have been too pessimistic about the possibility of gaining knowledge about pre-Pauline Christianity, but she rightly stressed that the present context is decisive in interpreting traditional material. Regarding Philippians 2:5–11 ("Philippians 2:6–11," in *Jesus und Paulus: Festschrift für W. G. Kümmel*, ed. E. E. Ellis and E. Grässer [Göttingen: Vandenhoeck und Ruprecht, 1975], 152), she said, "If the passage is *pre*-Pauline, then we have no guide-lines to help us in understanding its meaning. Commentators may speculate about the background—but we know very little about pre-Pauline Christianity, and nothing at all about the context in which the passage originated. It may therefore be more profitable to look first at the function of these verses in the present context and to enquire about possible parallels within Paul's own writings. For even if the material is non-Pauline, we may expect Paul himself to have interpreted it and used it in a Pauline manner." For similar skepticism regarding the attempt to detect the original form of the hymn, see G. F. Hawthorne, *Philippians* (Waco: Word, 1983), 77, and W. G. Kümmel, *Introduction to the New Testament*, rev. ed. (Nashville: Abingdon, 1975), 334–35. Kümmel said, "It is not clear up to the present moment by what formal standards we are to reconstruct an early Christian hymn, so that the separating out of the Pauline additions from the traditional text on the basis of formal criteria is extremely uncertain," and, "nothing compels the conclusion that Paul himself could not have formulated this hymn on the basis of such tradition" (p. 335).

25. For a survey of scholarship, see P. T. O'Brien, *Colossians, Philemon* (Waco: Word, 1982), 37–40.

26. E. Schweizer, *The Letter to the Colossians* (Minneapolis: Augsburg, 1982), 58–63.

Christ was "the head of the body," and by "body" the original author meant "universe." So the original hymn said that Christ was the head of the cosmos or universe. The author of Colossians changed the meaning of the hymn by stressing that Christ was the head of the body, that is, the church.

Schweizer was possibly correct in his analysis of the original text of the hymn. But two points can be made in response to his reconstruction. First, his alleged reconstruction does not change the meaning of the present text of Colossians 1:15–20, although the additions would indicate, if Schweizer were correct, the author's emphases in the hymn. Second, the fact that no agreement has been reached on the *Ur-text* of the hymn or on its poetic structure shows that this enterprise is very speculative. Kümmel rightly said:

> But the numerous reconstructions of the hymn expanded by the author that have been undertaken since Lohmeyer's analysis have scarcely led to a really convincing result. Indeed, the assumption is not yet proved that a *hymn* constructed according to a strict scheme has been used and that accordingly every fragment of a sentence beyond the scheme must stem from the author of Col. What is far more likely is that the author of Col himself has formed the hymn, utilizing traditional material; by this line of reasoning, the oft-repeated assumption that the cosmic statements of the hymn have by the addition of τῆς ἐκκλησίας (1:18) been transmuted into churchly statements is completely unproved.[27]

In examining traditional materials in Pauline literature, the interpreter should establish the interpretation from the existing context and beware of imposing speculative theories onto the text. Nevertheless, this does not mean that trying to recover pre-Pauline Christianity from traditional materials in Paul has no value, for such study may succeed in showing antecedents to Pauline thought in Palestinian Christianity.

Occasional Nature of Paul's Letters

One of the most crucial points to remember in interpreting Paul's letters is that they were written to address specific situations. They are not systematic treatises that were intended to

27. *Introduction to the New Testament*, 343.

present a complete Christian theology. They are pastoral works in which Paul applied his theology to specific problems in the churches. Romans and Ephesians are probably exceptions to this. In them Paul seemed to describe more generally and comprehensively his understanding of the Christian gospel; however, even these letters are not comprehensive treatises.[28] For example, Romans has no extended teaching on the church and no reference to the eucharist.

Several examples will reveal the circumstantial nature of the letters. Clearly Paul wrote Galatians because the Galatian churches were abandoning Paul's gospel (Gal. 1:6ff.; 5:2–6). He wrote Colossians to stave off a new heresy that had the potential of making inroads in the church (Col. 2:4–23). Various problems plagued the Corinthian church, and thus Paul wrote our two canonical letters to them. Philippians seems to have been written for several reasons. The church had sent Paul a gift and he wanted to express his thanks (1:3ff.; 4:10ff.). In addition, disunity was probably surfacing in the church (1:27–2:11; 4:2–3), and Paul wanted to warn the church regarding the danger of false teachers (3:2–4:1). All of the Pastoral letters (1–2 Timothy, Titus) were written to strengthen churches in healthy teaching because false teaching was threatening the churches.

The danger of reading Paul's letters as systematic treatises is that one might conclude too much from reading only one letter. For example, John Drane thought that Paul was a libertine in Galatians and a legalist in 1 Corinthians, since in the former Paul trumpeted liberty from law and in the latter Paul laid down many specific rulings.[29] Drane would certainly claim that he did not read the letters as systematic treatises; nevertheless, he has failed to see that Paul stressed liberty in

28. R. N. Longenecker ("On the Form, Function, and Authority of the New Testament Letters," in *Scripture and Truth*, ed. D. A. Carson and J. D. Woodbridge [Grand Rapids: Zondervan, 1983], 104–5) may have been correct in seeing Romans and Ephesians as letters that are not as clearly addressed to specific situations. He called them "tractate" letters. On the other hand, some scholars contend that Romans was also written to address a specific situation. For a discussion of the purpose and nature of Romans, see *The Romans Debate*, ed. K. P. Donfried (Minneapolis: Augsburg, 1977). Cf. also J. D. G. Dunn, *Romans* (Waco: Word, 1988), 1:xv–xviii, xliii; P. S. Minear, *The Obedience of Faith: The Purposes of Paul in the Epistle to the Romans* (Naperville, Ill.: Allenson, 1971).

29. John Drane, *Paul: Libertine or Legalist? A Study of the Theology of the Major Pauline Epistles* (London: SPCK, 1975).

Galatians because he was writing to a church that was infected with legalism, and Paul highlighted obedience in 1 Corinthians because he was writing to a church that gave full license to immoral behavior.[30] Neither in Galatians nor in 1 Corinthians did Paul explain his full view of Christian obedience. Instead, he gave "change of course" directions to churches that were navigating in the wrong direction.

The interpreter, then, must always keep in mind the specific situation that Paul was addressing in his letters. Of course, one can find out what this situation was only by reading the letter itself. All we know about the adversaries in Galatians appears in the letter to the Galatians. We are at some disadvantage here because the Galatian churches understood perfectly the problem that Paul was addressing; they were experiencing it! Paul did not write the letter to those of us who live in the 20th century. We can only infer from the evidence that we find in Paul's letters the precise nature of the problem in the churches to which he wrote. Morna Hooker has pointed out that hearing only Paul's response to the problems is much like hearing only one end of a telephone conversation.[31] Despite this disadvantage the interpreter is wise who reconstructs from the letter itself the situation that was plaguing the church. Then the Pauline response can be grasped more clearly.

In trying to reconstruct the situation that Paul addressed, interpreters often lack consensus on what problem confronted Paul, or even if there was a problem. For example, according to J. J. Gunther, scholars have made 44 different identifications of the opponents in Colossae.[32] And Morna Hooker doubted that there were any opponents at all.[33] Scholars have identified the adversaries in Galatia as gnostics, libertines, judaizing legalists, etc. Such debates are typical of each one of the Pauline letters. Such a diversity of opinions causes one to wonder if it is even possible to identify the opponents or

30. For the same criticism, see D. A. Carson, "Unity and Diversity in the New Testament: The Possibility of Systematic Theology," in *Scripture and Truth*, ed. D. A. Carson and J. D. Woodbridge (Grand Rapids: Zondervan, 1983), 87.

31. M. D. Hooker, "Were There False Teachers in Colossae?" in *Christ and Spirit in the New Testament*, ed. B. Lindars and S. S. Smalley (Cambridge: Cambridge University Press, 1973), 315.

32. J. J. Gunther, *St. Paul's Opponents and Their Background. A Study of Apocalyptic and Jewish Sectarian Teachings* (Leiden: Brill, 1973), 3–4.

33. "False Teachers in Colossae?" 315–31.

the specific situation that Paul addressed. Almost all would agree that Paul wrote his letters to confront specific problems, but can we identify those problems?

Examples from 1 Thessalonians and Galatians may help here. On the one hand, Paul's emphasis on the integrity of his ministry in 1 Thessalonians 2:1–12 has often been taken as an indication that he was responding to opponents who criticized him on this count. Advocates of this position maintain that the reason Paul defended the integrity of his ministry with such vigor was that the adversaries in Thessalonica had questioned his apostolic authority on this very point.

On the other hand, a more likely position is that Paul's defense of his ministry may be due to rhetorical purposes.[34] There is no indication anywhere else in 1 Thessalonians that Paul was responding to opponents who were attacking his apostleship. And Paul is clearly happy with the progress of the Christian community. He rejoiced over their vibrant faith, which was strong despite the afflictions they endured. He simply wanted them to progress further in the faith (1:2–10; 3:6–10; 4:1–2). It is interesting to note as a confirming argument that 1 Thessalonians 1:1 is one of the few openings where Paul did not identify himself as an apostle. This suggests that the legitimacy of Paul's apostleship was not in question here, especially when we compare 1 Thessalonians with other letters where Paul's apostleship was being questioned (1 Cor. 1:1; 2 Cor. 1:1; Gal. 1:1). In all of these other letters Paul affirmed his apostolic authority from the very beginning.[35]

To read Paul's defense of his ministry as a response to opponents is to practice what is called *mirror* reading. In this case one could argue that since Paul was defending his

34. For a defense of this view, see A. J. Malherbe, "'Gentle as a Nurse': The Cynic Background to 1 Thess. 2," *Novum Testamentum* 12 (1970): 203–13; *idem*, "Exhortation in First Thessalonians," *Novum Testamentum* 25 (1983): 238–56; Lyons, *Pauline Autobiography*, 177–221. I am not convinced regarding the Cynic background of 1 Thessalonians 2, nor has Lyons proved, in my estimation, his particular rhetorical understanding of the letter. But both of these scholars are correct in principle when they assert that Paul's defense in 1 Thessalonians 2 may function as a support of his gospel rather than as an indication that some were opposing Paul's gospel.

35. This is not to claim that if Paul mentions his apostleship, then the validity of his apostleship is being questioned. We are simply noting that *if* Paul's apostleship is being questioned, and such doubts about the genuineness of his apostleship are evident in the rest of the letter, then Paul invariably asserts his apostleship in the greeting. Of course, it is possible that 1 Thessalonians could be the exception to this observation, and that is why I said this was a confirmatory argument rather than a decisive one.

integrity, some opponents must have been questioning it; however, the conclusion does not necessarily follow from the premise. Paul was probably appealing to his behavior because his behavior functioned as a parenetic example for the Thessalonians. Paul's sustained defense of himself was intended to amplify his argument, and it does not necessarily suggest that he was responding to opponents. He reminded the Thessalonians that his behavior was above reproach, and his godly conduct testified that the gospel came with the power of the Holy Spirit (1 Thess. 1:5, 9; 2:1). Of course, it is possible that Paul was responding to the accusations of opponents. The point I am trying to make here is that the interpreter should at least beware of assuming that if Paul defended his apostleship, then it necessarily follows that some were attacking it. It is also possible that Paul's self-defense functions as part of the parenetical thrust of 1 Thessalonians.

Another example occurs in the letter to the Galatians. The majority of scholars still see the opponents as Judaizers, and they deduce that Paul was defending his apostleship from attack in chapters 1 and 2. In a recent dissertation, however, Lyons maintained that such a view is another example of inappropriate mirror reading.[36] Paul's long narrative section in these chapters is not designed to defend himself against opponents. Lyons claimed that Paul was using a typical example of autobiographical narrative in these chapters in order to set forth himself as an example of the Christian freedom that he wanted his readers to embrace.[37] Because Paul was an apostle, he was inseparably tied to the message of the gospel that he preached.

Lyons understood Galatians 1:10–2:21 to be a rhetorical unit of Greco-Roman autobiographical writing. He divided the autobiographical narrative into five sections: (1) 1:10–12 is the introduction in which Paul maintained the divine origin of his gospel; (2) 1:13–17 focuses on "Paul's ethos"; the former persecutor of the church has now become a preacher of the gospel; (3) Paul's conduct in different localities, especially Jerusalem, comes to the fore in 1:18–2:10; (4) 2:11–20 functions as a comparison of Paul and Cephas; and (5) 2:21 is the conclusion to this section.

36. *Pauline Autobiography*, 96–112.
37. Ibid.

In summary, reading Galatians to identify the opponents is to miss the point. According to Lyons, a better way is to recognize the rhetorical argumentation that is present in the letter.

Before we evaluate Lyons' thesis, we should pause to make several observations about methodology. I have been suggesting that the careful interpreter of the Pauline letters will try to understand these letters in the light of the specific situations that provoked the letter. But we have run up against the problem of trying to identify precisely the situations that Paul was addressing. How do we know if Paul was responding to a problem in the congregation or whether what we have in the letter is simply a part of Paul's argument? At this point two methodological questions can help the interpreter.[38] First, the interpreter should ask, Did Paul say anything *explicitly* about the opponents in his letter? This criterion is not fail-safe, and probably no criteria can establish the situation of Pauline communities with absolute certainty. However, since Paul said nothing about any adversaries *within* the church in 1 Thessalonians, it is likely that there were none. On the other hand, he explicitly mentioned in Galatians (1:6–9; see also 3:1; 5:10, 12; 6:12) that some at Galatia were preaching another gospel. We can clearly ascertain from the inclusion of these verses in Galatians that this is the major problem in the letter. In fact, Paul explicitly said in 6:12 that they were proclaiming circumcision.

Second, the interpreter should ask, Can any inferences about the opposition be plausibly drawn from the rest of the letter? This is obviously more precarious and uncertain, yet the interpreter can plausibly come to some conclusions from what the letter implies. It would be too skeptical to eliminate entirely this procedure. If Paul *frequently* mentions a particular issue, and does so with *urgency* and *clarity*, then one may justly conclude that he is speaking against opponents. Now this too is not a fail-safe criterion, but the presence of these features in a letter may tell us much about the opponents. This is especially true if Paul has already specifically indicated that there are opponents of some kind.

38. My discussion on mirror reading has been significantly influenced by J. M. G. Barclay, "Mirror Reading a Polemical Letter: Galatians as a Test Case," *Journal for the Study of the New Testament* 31 (1987): 73–93.

Let us return to Galatians as an example. Since Paul explicitly said that there were opponents, since we know that they preached circumcision, and since we know that the congregation was considering submission to circumcision (5:2–6), we may justly infer from Paul's long discussion on the role of the law in Galatians (2:15–4:31) that the opponents based their argument on the OT Scriptures. Paul had to contest their interpretation of the OT in order to convince the Galatians that circumcision was unnecessary to be part of the people of God.

What can we say about the autobiographical section of Galatians 1–2? Is this a rhetorical argument (Lyons), or were the opponents questioning the validity of Paul's apostleship? To pass judgment on this issue is more difficult since we are arguing from inferences. It is not clear to me, however, that Lyons was correct in his own rhetorical analysis of the section. Lyons did not successfully explain why Paul recounted in such detail his activities in different localities (Gal. 1:18–2:10). Also, several items in this section indicate that Paul was responding to those who argued that his apostleship was dependent upon Jerusalem. Paul emphasized that he saw *only* Peter and James on his first visit to Jerusalem (1:18–19), and then he affirmed that he was not lying (1:20). This last statement indicates that Paul anticipated some people would say he was not being truthful. Paul said emphatically that those in Judea did not know him personally (1:22–24). Why would he stress his relative obscurity in Jerusalem and Judea if Lyons was correct in saying that this section focuses on Paul's conduct? What function do these trivial statements have in the argument of the letter in Lyons' view? That they are part of Paul's apostolic self-defense makes the best sense. This deduction is strengthened by the fact that Galatians is the only book in which Paul explicitly defended his apostleship from the inception of the book (1:1). Furthermore, in 2:3–5 Paul mentioned false brothers who opposed his gospel and maintained that Titus should be circumcised. This is precisely the same problem that the Galatians faced, which we discover later in the letter (5:2–6; 6:12–16).

Lastly, it seems highly doubtful that Lyons was correct in identifying the genre of this section. We have already seen that describing 1:18–2:10 as Paul's conduct does not really explain the specific content of this section. Is the focus of 1:13–17 on "Paul's ethos?" Instead, the section seems to show the divine origination of his gospel. Also, the suggestion that the main burden of 2:11–20 is a comparison of Peter and Paul is unsatisfactory. Rather, the text stresses that Peter knew (εἰδότες, 2:16) that Paul's understanding of the gospel was correct. Peter's temporary fear of displeasing the circumcision party contradicted his own theological beliefs which were in accord with Paul's.

Lyons was right in criticizing some mirror reading because it can impose an alien understanding upon the Pauline letters. But rhetorical criticism poses a similar danger. Instead of allowing the letters to speak their distinctive messages, alien forms are often imposed on the letters.

Our main point here is that if opponents (as well as their beliefs) or problems are either explicitly named or sufficiently described in a letter, then the interpreter may justifiably draw more specific conclusions about other parts of the letter. Regarding the procedure of identifying specific opponents in a letter, several things can be said to avoid inappropriate mirror reading.

First, one should not postulate more than one opponent unless the evidence compels one to do so. The simpler hypothesis should be preferred over the more complex one.

Second, it is precarious to identify certain phrases or words as slogans or sayings of the opponents. For example, there is simply not enough evidence to conclude that the phrase "law of Christ" (Gal. 6:2) stems from the opponents. Yet there is some justification for seeing allusions to slogans in 1 Corinthians. For example, when Paul said, "It is good for a man not to touch a woman" (1 Cor. 7:1), he may have been citing a slogan contained in a letter that the Corinthians had written to him. Here the best counsel is caution, since speculation can run rampant in such an enterprise.

Third, the interpreter should be cautious in describing or identifying opponents from the parenetic section of a letter.[39] Many interpreters have seen libertines in Galatia because Paul warned against abusing liberty (see Gal. 5:13–6:10).

39. See P. Vielhauer, *Literatur,* 50, 57.

Such a conclusion is unlikely because nothing else in the letter suggests that the problem was libertinism. It is more probable in this part of the letter that Paul anticipated a possible *overreaction* to his teaching on liberty in Christ. After all, Paul was a wise pastor who foresaw a possible extreme in the congregation. On the other hand, in Colossians 2:4–23 Paul did seem to direct parenetical advice against specific opponents. Here Paul warned the community about alien philosophy, the worship of angels, and ascetic practices; however, it is very unlikely that the parenesis in Colossians 3:1–4:6 indicates any specific problems in Colossae, since the exhortations are very general in this latter section.

Fourth, the interpreter should resist the temptation to identify the opponents too precisely (e.g., with some other religious entity, such as Gnosticism,[40] the Qumran movement, Pharisaic Judaism, etc.). However, specific identifications should not be ruled out a priori. For example, the opponents in Galatians do seem remarkably similar to the believers mentioned in Acts 15:1–5. Nonetheless, attempts to identify the opponents with a religious-historical parallel often end up importing evidence from the outside into the letter. As an example, a few affinities are perceived between Gnosticism and 1 Corinthians, and then the entire problem in 1 Corinthians is described as Gnostic. Such identifications, however, often go beyond the evidence provided in the letter.

In conclusion, the student should recognize the literary nature of letters when interpreting the Pauline letters. He or she should generally expect the Pauline letters to contain a careful structure. Also, the student should identify any particular literary features and forms (such as the diatribe) that are present. Most important, the student should try to identify (from the letter itself) the situation or problem that provoked Paul to write to the congregation. A cautious reconstruction of the situation will grant the interpreter a more profound understanding of Paul's letters. Furthermore, a recognition of the circumstantial or situational nature of Paul's letters should discourage the reader from expecting Paul to give a

40. In fact, the nature of "Gnosticism" in the 1st century A.D. cannot be established precisely. See E. Yamauchi, *Pre-Christian Gnosticism*, 2d ed. (Grand Rapids: Baker, 1983).

complete and definitive exposition of every topic he addresses. However, in a sense we have gotten ahead of ourselves.
Prior to identifying the genre of a letter or determining the
situation it addresses, we must establish the correct text. We
turn to that topic in the next chapter.

2

Doing Textual Criticism

Before one starts interpreting a specific passage or letter, the correct text for that passage or letter should be established. I shall not explain in this chapter the basic philosophy, principles, and methods of textual criticism. A helpful introductory essay on establishing the text is contained in the introductory volume of this series, and I recommend that students follow the procedure suggested by Michael Holmes in that essay.[1] In this chapter I will make a few suggestions regarding textual study and highlight a few examples of the practice of textual criticism in Pauline literature.

Most students will probably not become experts in textual criticism, but at the very least they should avail themselves of B. M. Metzger's *A Textual Commentary on the Greek New Testament*.[2] In it Metzger recorded the reflections of the committee who edited the 3d edition of the United Bible Societies' Greek New Testament. As a result this tool enables the student to see why the committee preferred one reading over another. With the publication of this valuable tool even the student unskilled in textual criticism can identify the most crucial variants in the text.

Students should also learn how to use the textual appara-

1. M. W. Holmes, "New Testament Textual Criticism," in *Introducing New Testament Interpretation*, ed. Scot McKnight (Grand Rapids: Baker, 1989), 53–74. Holmes' essay also refers to other works in textual criticism for the student who wants to pursue the area further.

2. Corrected ed. (New York: United Bible Societies, 1975).

tus in both the Nestle-Aland and the United Bible Societies'
texts. The Nestle-Aland text lists more textual variants than
the United Bible Societies' text, and thus exposes the student
to variant readings not listed in the other text and not discussed in Metzger's *Commentary*.

Even variants that are clearly incorrect can help in interpretation because they can show how ancient scribes understood the passage. For example, 1 Corinthians 11:10 says that
"a woman ought to have authority [ἐξουσία] upon her head
because of the angels." What Paul means by "authority"
(ἐξουσία) here is perplexing. Early scribes puzzled over what
this meant as well, and thus in some early MSS the word
κάλυμμα ("veil") replaces ἐξουσία ("authority"). Although
clearly secondary and inferior, the word "veil" was inserted to
make the passage clearer and because it harmonized with the
injunction in verses 5–6 and 13 to wear head coverings. Thus,
verse 10 was changed so that it read "A woman ought to have
a veil upon her head because of the angels." All scholars today
agree that the word "authority" is the correct reading here,
but the use of the word "veil" in some MSS compels the interpreter to ask whether the early "interpretation" of this passage is valid. Of course, my purpose here is not to arbitrate
the interpretive debate over this verse. The point is that early
and inferior readings indicate how earlier interpreters understood the text, and the student should note these variants and
wrestle with such possible interpretations.

Students of the NT are familiar with the tendency of
scribes to harmonize parallel passages in the Gospels.
Harmonization is not as common in Paul since his letters
have fewer parallel passages. Nevertheless, the same tendency
toward harmonization manifests itself in parallel Pauline
texts. Ephesians 1:7 says that in Christ "we have redemption
through his blood, the forgiveness of trespasses." Colossians
1:14 is almost an exact parallel, for it says that in Christ "we
have redemption, the forgiveness of sins." Given the close parallel in Ephesians, it is not surprising that in Colossians some
scribes added "through his blood" after the word "redemption." Nevertheless, this variant reading in Colossians 1:14
was not in the original text, and was added either deliberately
to harmonize with the Ephesian text, or accidentally by a
scribe who had memorized this verse from Ephesians and

inadvertently inserted "through his blood" into the Colossians text.

The use and meaning of pronouns can often be significant in Pauline literature.[3] Differentiating between readings that favor ὑμεῖς or ἡμεῖς is extraordinarily difficult at times because scribes could easily confuse the two pronouns, especially since the words are so close in pronunciation. For example, in Colossians 1:7 does Paul call Epaphras "a faithful minister of Christ on *your* behalf" (ὑπὲρ ὑμῶν), or does he say that Epaphras is "a faithful minister of Christ on *our* behalf" (ὑπὲρ ἡμῶν)? The textual evidence points to the former, while the context suggests the latter. The intention here is not to resolve this question but to underscore the fact that the modern interpreter must carefully evaluate the textual evidence for variant readings. A similar problem is found in Romans 5:1 where the better textual witnesses read ἔχωμεν ("*let us have* peace with God"), but the context seems to favor ἔχομεν ("*we have* peace with God"). The variant readings here are probably due to the similar pronunciation of the vowels o and ω in *koine* Greek. Nevertheless, the exegetical difference here is significant, and an interpreter's decision on this question will inform one's understanding of the entire passage.

We should also note that minuscule 1739, although it is a 10th-century MS, is of high quality in Paul. It stands in the same stream of textual tradition as 𝔓[46] and B, which are Alexandrian MSS of high quality. Thus, readings that are supported by 𝔓[46], 1739, and B are usually original.[4]

We should note several significant examples in the practice of textual criticism in the Pauline letters so that the student can see the importance of textual criticism for exegesis. First, the words ἐν Ἐφέσῳ are missing in a number of important MSS, including the significant MSS we discussed above (𝔓[46], B, 1739) and Sinaiticus (ℵ). This strongly supports the theory that Ephesians was originally an encyclical letter, being sent to a number of churches in Asia Minor of which the Ephesian church was the most important. The encyclical theory would

---

3. C. E. B. Cranfield, "Changes in Person and Number in Paul's Epistles," in *Paul and Paulinism: Essays in Honour of C. K. Barrett* (London: SPCK, 1982), 280–89.

4. For an in-depth discussion of this point, see G. Zuntz, *The Text of the Epistles* (London: Oxford University Press, 1953), 56–84. Zuntz (pp. 158–59) thought that Western witnesses joined by 𝔓[46], B, and 1739 are more often right than wrong and that late witnesses may be superior when supported by 𝔓[46] and B.

explain the impersonal quality apparent in the letter, which is hard to explain if Paul were writing exclusively to the church at Ephesus where he had spent a considerable amount of time (see Acts 19). In this instance, how one views the textual evidence in Ephesians 1:1 will clearly influence how one conceives of the letter as a whole, that is, whether it is a specific letter to Ephesus or a more general tractate to a number of churches.

Second, the importance of textual criticism is also illustrated in the textual history of the ending of Romans, a passage entangled with all sorts of problems. T. W. Manson made the interesting suggestion that Romans 16 was not originally part of the letter to the Romans, but that another copy of Romans was sent to Ephesus and chapter 16 was attached to that version of Romans.[5] The omission in a few MSS of ἐν Ῥώμῃ in 1:7 and 1:15 also strengthens Manson's thesis. Such an analysis of the textual evidence fits with Manson's thesis that Romans contains a summary of Paul's theology found in his past conflicts. However, the recent work of H. Gamble contains strong arguments supporting the hypothesis that Romans 16 was sent to Rome,[6] and the student should consult this volume for a thorough discussion of the entire question. Gamble thought that the inclusion of chapter 16 in the letter to Rome made it more likely that Romans was addressed to a specific situation in Rome. We should say, however, that Gamble's theory regarding the occasion for Romans is permitted but not demanded from his analysis of the textual evidence of Romans 16.

Third, the final doxology of Romans (Rom. 16:25–27) is also textually questionable. Among its variants are: (1) its omission in some MSS; (2) its placement after Romans 14:23 in others; (3) its occurrence after Romans 15:33 in 𝔓[46]; and (4) its insertion after both 14:23 and 15:33 in minuscule 1506 but omission after 16:24. Still other MSS include the passage after both 14:23 and 16:24. Some scholars have also voiced doubts about the authenticity of the doxology, due to the omission of the typical benediction at the close of the letter,

5. See his "St. Paul's Letter to the Romans—and Others," *Bulletin of the John Rylands Library* 31 (1948): 224–40.

6. H. Gamble, *The Textual History of the Letter to the Romans* (Grand Rapids: Eerdmans, 1977).

the alleged Marcionite character of the text (the revelation of the "mystery" [v. 25] is alleged to be gnostic), and a doxology that is atypically long for Paul.

Nevertheless, we can offer strong arguments that support the authenticity of Romans 16:25–27, and it is also probable that the passage is correctly inserted after 16:24. The external textual evidence is strongest for inclusion after 16:24. Textual witnesses such as $\mathfrak{P}^{61}$, $\aleph$, B, C, D, 81, 1739, and others support the insertion of the text here. Thus, significant Alexandrian and some Western evidence suggest that the doxology concludes the epistle.

In my opinion, internal evidence also supports the authenticity of the text. It is not surprising that Romans ends with a long doxology because the same letter also contains the longest greeting and opening found in all the Pauline letters (1:1–7). Indeed, a careful reading of Romans shows that a number of themes in the opening are picked up again in the doxology, for example, the obedience of faith among the Gentiles (see 1:5; 16:26), and that the gospel is in accord with the Scriptures (see 1:2; 16:26). A long doxology is appropriate in what is undoubtedly Paul's most theologically significant letter. That the passage is Marcionite is unlikely since the text asserts continuity with the OT Scriptures, and the revelation of the mystery is not gnostic, for Paul speaks elsewhere of the gospel as a mystery now revealed (Col. 1:24ff.; Eph. 3:2ff.). The lack of a "grace" benediction concluding the letter is the strongest argument for inauthenticity, but its probable insertion after 16:20 shows that the benediction did not end the letter in any case.

3

Translating and Analyzing the Letter

Translating

After establishing the correct text the student should translate the letter (or passage) being investigated. The goal at this point is to have a good working knowledge of the text. Subsequent detailed exegesis may lead the student to revise the initial translation. For translation the student should use the lexicon by Bauer, Arndt, and Gingrich.[1] This resource contains a wealth of information. Not only does it provide word definitions, but it also provides information on the history of a word, suggests interpretations and translations of difficult constructions, and gives bibliography for further study. Every serious student of the NT should own and habitually use this indispensable tool.

One problem faced by beginning students is navigating their way around BAGD. Of course, constant use is the key to becoming more familiar with the tool. But too much frustration can produce despair and some students give up altogether. Fortunately, an index is available that helps the student

---

1. W. Bauer, *A Greek-English Lexicon of the New Testament and Other Early Christian Literature*, trans. and adapted by W. F. Arndt and F. W. Gingrich, 2d ed. rev. and augmented by F. W. Gingrich and F. W. Danker (Chicago: University of Chicago Press, 1979). Hereafter referred to as BAGD.

locate the discussions in BAGD of Greek words as they appear in the verses of the Greek NT.[2] The index is especially invaluable when attempting to locate the treatment of a certain word within a long entry in BAGD (e.g., certain prepositions). On the other hand, an overdependence on the index may rob the student of certain riches discovered only by rummaging around in the pages and entries of BAGD.

I have found that one of the greatest weaknesses of students is an inability to read the Greek NT. They can do capable exegesis, but their lack of reading ability in Greek requires that they spend excessive time translating the text. These students should engage in a program of regular reading to improve their ability to read the Greek text with greater speed. Students who do not feel comfortable reading the Greek text rarely engage in the exegesis of it. I have found that the best tool for rapid reading of the Greek NT is *A Grammatical Analysis of the Greek New Testament* by M. Zerwick and M. Grosvenor.[3] This book contains an analysis of the entire NT in canonical order. It parses difficult forms and gives invaluable help on grammatical constructions. In addition, a preface contains parsing tables and a useful review of Greek grammar. Moreover, this work is keyed to Zerwick's intermediate Greek grammar, which is a valuable work in its own right.[4]

A book similar to Zerwick's in style and format is F. Rienecker's *A Linguistic Key to the Greek New Testament*.[5] However, I would recommend Zerwick above Rienecker, since Zerwick's volume contains more grammatical help, whereas Rienecker comments more extensively on the meaning of words. Students can also profit from using *A Reader's Greek-English Lexicon of the New Testament and a Beginner's Guide for the Translation of New Testament Greek* by Sakae Kubo.[6] It

2. J. R. Alsop, *An Index to the Revised Bauer-Arndt-Gingrich Greek Lexicon*, 2d rev. ed. (Grand Rapids: Zondervan, 1981).

3. M. Zerwick and M. Grosvenor, *A Grammatical Analysis of the Greek New Testament*, rev. ed. (Rome: Biblical Institute Press, 1981).

4. M. Zerwick, *Biblical Greek Illustrated by Examples*, trans. J. P. Smith (Rome: Biblical Institute Press, 1963).

5. F. Rienecker, *A Linguistic Key to the Greek New Testament* (Grand Rapids: Zondervan, 1981).

6. S. Kubo, *A Reader's Greek-English Lexicon of the New Testament and a Beginner's Guide for the Translation of New Testament Greek* (Grand Rapids: Zondervan, 1975).

assumes that the reader has a knowledge of all words that occur fifty times or more in the Greek NT, although an appendix in the back of the book contains all of these words. The heart of the book proceeds through the NT in canonical order, listing under the appropriate chapter and verse each word that occurs less than fifty times in the NT. Any word that occurs six times or more in a particular book but less than fifty times in the NT is listed as special vocabulary at the beginning of that book. A brief review of beginning Greek is also found at the back of the book. If the student can afford to buy only one tool, my recommendation is Zerwick and Grosvenor.

Parsing

The student should not rely upon parsing guides, for the one who does will never learn to parse with confidence. Ultimately, one *will* save time by learning the forms! Nevertheless, there is no great virtue in spending a great amount of time in figuring out a form when one gets stuck. These guides can also help a student who wants to check his or her parsing, although we must warn that these guides are not inerrant!

I will cover these guides in the order that I recommend them. The *Analytical Greek New Testament* edited by Barbara and Timothy Friberg is the best aid available for the student.[7] The entire Greek NT is printed in canonical order and the parsing of each Greek word is listed beneath as an analytical "tag," using a system that is easily learned with a little practice. Another useful parsing tool is *The Analytical Greek Lexicon Revised* by H. K. Moulton.[8] All NT Greek forms are listed alphabetically and parsed. The root of each word is also given. *A Parsing Guide to the Greek New Testament* by N. E. Han identifies each verb in the NT.[9] Lastly, if a student would like to refer to a handbook of Greek forms, W. G. MacDonald

7. B. and T. Friberg, *Analytical Greek New Testament* (Grand Rapids: Baker Book House, 1981).

8. H. K. Moulton, *The Analytical Greek Lexicon Revised* (Grand Rapids: Zondervan, 1978).

9. N. E. Han, *A Parsing Guide to the Greek New Testament* (Scottsdale, Pa.: Herald, 1971).

provided a clear and usable review in a book entitled *Greek Enchiridon*.[10]

Interlinears

In conclusion, I should say a word about interlinears. I do not recommend interlinears because they usually become a substitute for reading the original text and ensure that one does not learn Greek. A better tool is the *Greek-English New Testament*.[11] This edition includes the RSV NT and the Nestle-Aland[26] text on facing pages.

10. W. G. MacDonald, *Greek Enchiridon* (Peabody, Mass.: Hendrickson, 1986).
11. 3d ed. (Stuttgart: Deutsche Bibelgesellschaft, 1986).

4

Investigating Historical and Introductory Issues

The investigation of historical and introductory issues could have been inserted at various places in this book. I have decided to include the chapter at this point for two reasons. First, unlike other parts of the exegetical process, a broad understanding of the Greco-Roman world, and Jewish culture and history in particular, is a general task that is not so much related to any particular passage as it is to the acquiring of a broad perspective of the culture and history of the time. This step, in other words, can be placed about anywhere in the process since it is not a distinct step per se. The student should continue to read broadly in this area in order to become familiar with the culture and history of the NT era. Second, before the modern reader plunges into a detailed exegesis of a letter, it is helpful to read an introduction on that letter. The major issues that have been discussed in critical scholarship will then be apparent to the reader. There is no particular virtue in reading the letter uninformed about the critical issues in the letter. In fact, knowledge of these critical issues will make it possible for the student to interact with the letter more intelligently.

This chapter can be divided into two segments. The first part will focus on historical-cultural issues. Here we will concentrate on books that are helpful in opening up the historical context for the reader. The second part will focus on introductory issues that relate specifically to the book under consideration, that is, questions of authorship, date, integrity, and other critical issues.

General Historical-Cultural Background

The more one knows about the culture, history, and literature of NT times, the greater will be the ability to put oneself into the shoes of the original readers, which is always a benefit in interpretation. After all, Paul was not writing to our own 20th-century culture, but to a culture that existed nearly 2000 years ago. The language barrier alone indicates the cultural gap between Paul and present-day readers.

Some scholars who stress the importance of literary criticism or rhetorical criticism rule out the importance of historical-cultural study. For them the literary dimension of the text is the only important factor in interpretation. The problem with this view is that it often separates the author from the text, giving the text a life of its own apart from the author. It also dissociates the author from the culture and world in which the author lived.[1] Radical literary perspectives banish the author and exclude any normativity in interpretation. Such an ahistorical and nihilistic approach should be rejected.[2] To eliminate historical study is self-defeating since the historical study of words contributes significantly toward understanding the meaning of an author's words. In other words, studying the meaning of a term in ancient documents written by various authors can clarify the meaning of that same term in another author's document.

Indeed, we are keenly aware of historical limitation when reading a passage like 2 Thessalonians 2:6–7. There Paul reminded the Thessalonians that they knew what was restraining the man of lawlessness. The Thessalonians knew what was preventing the arrival of the lawless one because Paul had orally instructed them on this topic (2 Thess. 2:5).

1. For valuable critiques of this literary approach, see the three articles in *Trinity Journal* 8 (1987): C. F. H. Henry, "Narrative Theology: An Evangelical Appraisal," 3–19; K. J. Vanhoozer, "A Lamp in the Labyrinth: The Hermeneutics of 'Aesthetic' Theology," 25–56; and S. McKnight, "Literary Criticism of the Synoptic Gospels," 57–68.

2. On the other hand, J. H. Sailhamer ("Exegesis of the Old Testament as a Text," in *A Tribute to Gleason Archer*, ed. W. C. Kaiser, Jr., and R. F. Youngblood [Chicago: Moody, 1986], 279–93) rightly cautioned that extrabiblical historical data should not control the interpretation of the text in such a way that it takes precedence over the actual composition and wording of a text by an author.

Apparently, Paul could safely assume that the identity of the restrainer was common knowledge among the Thessalonians; however, what was common knowledge for them remains unknown to the modern reader.[3]

Thus a historical and cultural gap is fixed between Paul and the modern reader. Yet the more the student reads, the better chance he or she has of bridging that gap. For the reader who desires to acquire a general sweep of NT history the following works are recommended:

E. Ferguson, *Backgrounds of Early Christianity* (Grand Rapids: Eerdmans, 1987). This book is the most helpful introduction and is remarkably comprehensive and concise. The bibliography will guide the student to more detailed study in each area. If the reader were to buy only one book, this is the one to get!

J. E. Stambaugh and D. L. Balch, *The New Testament in Its Social Environment* (Philadelphia: Westminster, 1986). A nontechnical introduction to the society and history of NT times.

F. F. Bruce, *New Testament History* (Garden City, N.Y.: Doubleday, 1969). Bruce consistently weaves the history of NT times into the larger fabric of the history of the Greco-Roman world, insofar as the latter pertains to NT history.

B. Reicke, *The New Testament Era: The World of the Bible from 500 B.C. to A.D. 100* (Philadelphia: Fortress, 1968). A lucid exposition of the history and background of NT times.

E. Lohse, *The New Testament Environment* (Nashville: Abingdon, 1976). Lohse does not discuss NT history but the historical context that relates to NT history.

The following two works contain excerpts from primary sources of the NT era:

C. K. Barrett, *The New Testament Background: Selected Documents*, rev. and expanded ed. (San Francisco: Harper & Row, 1989).

---

3. Of course, no amount of historical research will resolve this particular problem since Paul's oral communication with the Thessalonians is irrecoverable.

H. C. Kee, *The Origins of Christianity: Sources and Documents* (Englewood Cliffs, N.J.: Prentice-Hall, 1973).

After reading a survey of NT history, the student should plunge right into reading the primary sources. Nothing can replace the excitement of reading the primary sources first hand. The following primary sources are particularly recommended:

The Apocrypha of the Old Testament. Both the RSV and NEB have handy editions that contain the Apocrypha. The New American Bible is a readable translation by Roman Catholic scholars of the apocryphal books considered canonical by the Catholic church.

J. H. Charlesworth, ed., *The Old Testament Pseudepigrapha*, 2 vols. (Garden City, N.J.: Doubleday, 1983, 1985). For a concordance to the pseudepigrapha, see *Concordance Grecque des Pseudépigraphes D'Ancien Testament*, ed. A.-M. Denis and Y. Janssens (Leiden: Brill, 1987).

The Dead Sea Scrolls. The standard translation is by A. Dupont-Sommer, *The Essene Writings from Qumran* (Oxford: Blackwell, 1961; repr., Gloucester, Mass.: Peter Smith, 1973). For a handy English translation, see G. Vermes, *The Dead Sea Scrolls in English*, 3d ed. (New York: Penguin, 1987). For a concordance, see K. G. Kuhn, *Konkordanz zu den Qumrantexten* (Göttingen: Vandenhoeck & Ruprecht, 1960). Various issues of *Revue de Qumran* subsequent to 1960 contain updates for a concordance of the Dead Sea Scrolls.

For the Mishnah, see H. Danby, *The Mishnah* (Oxford: Oxford University Press, 1933). See also *The Mishnah: A New Translation*, tr. J. Neusner (New Haven: Yale University Press, 1988).

J. Neusner has now translated or edited all 6 volumes of *The Tosefta* (New York: Ktav, 1977–1986). The standard editions of the Babylonian Talmud and Midrashim are *The Babylonian Talmud*, 34 vols., ed. I. Epstein (London: Soncino, 1935–1952), and *Midrashim*, ed. H. Freedman and M. Simon, 5 vols. (London: Soncino, 1977).

For the Jewish historian Josephus, see the 10-volume set in the Loeb Classical Library (Harvard University Press);

for the writings of Philo see the 12-volume set in the
Loeb Classical Library.
Gnostic Writings: J. M. Robinson, ed., *The Nag Hammadi
Library*, rev. ed. (San Francisco: Harper & Row, 1988).

Secondary sources can also deepen a student's understanding of the literature found in primary sources. A student can
begin by consulting the resources listed below. For an annotated bibliography on the intertestamental period, see S. F.
Noll, *The Intertestamental Period: A Study Guide* (Downers
Grove, Ill.: InterVarsity, 1985). For an extensive bibliography
the student should consult J. A. Fitzmyer, *An Introductory
Bibliography for the Study of Scripture*, rev. ed. (Rome: Biblical
Institute Press, 1981), and N. E. Anderson, *Tools for Bibliographical and Backgrounds Research on the New Testament*, 2d
ed. (South Hamilton, Mass.: Gordon-Conwell Theological Seminary, 1987).

G. F. Moore, *Judaism in the First Century of the Christian
Era: The Age of the Tannaim*, 2 vols. (New York: Schocken,
1927, 1930). A classic work on Judaism.

J. Neusner, *Judaism: The Evidence of the Mishnah* (Chicago:
University of Chicago, 1981). Note this prolific author's
many works on Judaism, for example, *The Rabbinic
Traditions about the Pharisees Before 70 A.D.*, 3 vols.
(Leiden: E. J. Brill, 1971) and *From Politics to Piety: The
Emergence of Pharisaic Judaism* (Englewood Cliffs, N.J.:
Prentice-Hall, 1973).

M. Stern, *Greek and Latin Authors on Jews and Judaism*,
2 vols. (Jerusalem: Israel Academy of Sciences and
Humanities, 1974, 1980). E. E. Urbach, *The Sages: Their
Concepts and Beliefs*, 2 vols. (Jerusalem: Magnes, 1975).
Stern and Urbach are two helpful resources on Judaism.

E. Schürer, *The History of the Jewish People in the Age of
Jesus Christ*, ed. M. Black, G. Vermes, F. Millar, and
M. Goodman, 3 vols., rev. ed. (Edinburgh: T. & T. Clark,
1973–86). An invaluable work on the history of the Jews
in NT times.

S. Safrai and M. Stern, eds., *The Jewish People in The First
Century: Historical Geography, Political History, Social,
Cultural and Religious Life and Institutions* (Phila-

delphia: Fortress, 1974). This is the first volume of a multivolume work in an ongoing series entitled *Compendia Rerum Iudaicarum ad Novum Testamentum*. Although very similar to Schürer, it is less technical. The two volumes listed immediately below are also part of this series.

M. E. Stone, ed., *Jewish Writings of the Second Temple Period: Apocrypha, Pseudepigrapha, Qumran Sectarian Writings, Philo, Josephus* (Philadelphia: Fortress, 1984).

S. Safrai and P. J. Tomson, ed., *The Literature of the Sages. First Part: Oral Torah, Halakha, Mishna, Tosefta, Talmud, External Tractates* (Philadelphia: Fortress, 1987).

M. Hengel, *Judaism and Hellenism* (Philadelphia: Fortress, 1974). Disputes the idea that an absolute distinction can be maintained between Judaism and Hellenism.

R. H. Nash, *Christianity in the Hellenistic World* (Grand Rapids: Zondervan, 1984). Demonstrates that Christianity was not dependent upon or derived from the mystery religions or Gnosticism. One of the best texts for the beginning student.

J. Jeremias, *Jerusalem in the Time of Jesus: An Investigation into Economic and Social Conditions During the New Testament Period* (Philadelphia: Fortress, 1969). One needs to be cautious with this work, since Jeremias sometimes does not take into account the date of his sources.

For two introductions to Jewish literature see, G. W. E. Nickelsburg, *Jewish Literature Between the Bible and the Mishnah: An Historical and Literary Introduction* (Philadelphia: Fortress, 1981), and R. C. Musaph-Andriesse, *From Torah to Kabbalah: A Basic Introduction to the Writings of Judaism* (Oxford: Oxford University Press, 1982).

G. Vermes, *The Dead Sea Scrolls: Qumran in Perspective* (Philadelphia: Fortress, 1977). A fine introduction to the Dead Sea Scrolls.

H. Koester, *Introduction to the New Testament. History, Culture and Religion of the Hellenistic Age*, Vol. 1 (Philadelphia: Fortress, 1982). Helpful introduction to Hellenistic background.

K. Rudolph, *Gnosis: The Nature and History of Gnosticism* (San Francisco: Harper & Row, 1983). The classic work on Gnosticism.

E. M. Yamauchi, *Pre-Christian Gnosticism*, 2d ed. (Grand Rapids: Baker, 1983). This work demonstrates that second-century Gnosticism should not be read into first-century documents.

The recent interest in the relationship between sociology and the NT is already opening up some new perspectives on NT documents. No background study is sufficient any longer without a consideration of sociology. The recent nature of the discipline suggests that an interpreter should be cautious in using this material. Presumably more consensus will emerge as research continues. The first two books below provide concise introductions to the discipline for the reader.

H. C. Kee, *Christian Origins in Sociological Perspective* (Philadelphia: Westminster, 1980).

A. J. Malherbe, *Social Aspects of Early Christianity*, 2d ed. (Philadelphia: Fortress, 1983).

W. A. Meeks, *The First Urban Christians: The Social World of the Apostle Paul* (New Haven: Yale University Press, 1983). Meeks' book is probably the most important work from a sociological perspective on the Pauline letters.

G. Theissen, *The Social Setting of Pauline Christianity: Essays on Corinth* (Philadelphia: Fortress, 1982). This provocative work examines the sociological situation of the church in Corinth.

Scarcely anything has been done on the relationship between psychology and Pauline Christianity. A recent book by Theissen (*Psychological Aspects of Pauline Theology* [Philadelphia: Fortress, 1987]) may provoke others to launch out into this area. Obviously, such recent studies are controversial, but they should not be rejected out of hand, for psychology, properly used, gives the reader another perspective of the biblical text.

Other valuable resources on historical cultural issues include the many available Bible encyclopedias and dictionaries. These reference tools contain concise articles with bibliographies on historical, introductory, and theological issues. I think all students should have in their library at least *The Interpreter's Bible Dictionary* and *The International Standard Bible Encyclopedia*, rev. ed. (see below).

> *The New Bible Dictionary*, ed. J. D. Douglas, et al., 2d ed. (Wheaton: Tyndale, 1982). A fine one-volume dictionary for the student. *The Illustrated Bible Dictionary* has the same text as the one-volume edition, but has added beautiful photographs, full-color relief maps, charts, and other illustrative material.
>
> *The Interpreter's Bible Dictionary*, ed. G. A. Buttrick, 4 vols. (New York and Nashville: Abingdon, 1962). *Supplementary Volume*, ed. K. Crim (Nashville: Abingdon, 1976). A standard critical tool.
>
> *The International Standard Bible Encyclopedia*, ed. G. W. Bromiley, E. F. Harrison, R. K. Harrison, W. S. LaSor, and E. W. Smith, Jr., 4 vols. (Grand Rapids: Eerdmans, 1979–1987). Solid evangelical scholarship which will help balance some of the views found in *The Interpreter's Bible Dictionary*.
>
> *Zondervan Pictorial Encyclopedia of the Bible*, ed. M. C. Tenney, 5 vols. (Grand Rapids: Zondervan, 1975). This work reflects conservative evangelical scholarship.
>
> *Encylopedia Judaica*, ed. C. Roth, 16 vols. (Jerusalem: Macmillan, 1971–1972). A reference tool on contemporary and historical Judaism.
>
> *The Jewish Encyclopedia*, ed. I. Singer, 12 vols. (New York: Funk and Wagnalls, 1901–1906). Although older than the previous work, it contains much valuable information on Judaism that is not found in the former.
>
> M. Cary and T. J. Haarhoof, *Life and Thought in the Greek and Roman World* (London: Methuen, 1940). For an understanding of everyday life in the Greco-Roman world.
>
> *The Oxford Classical Dictionary*, ed. N. G. L. Hammond and H. H. Scullard, 2d ed. (London: Oxford University Press, 1970). Crucial tool for ancient Greek and Roman civilization.

Specific Historical-cultural Issues

Some passages in the epistles will raise questions about specific historical cultural issues. For example, What was slavery like in the Greco-Roman world? What kind of clothing did women wear in antiquity (see 1 Tim. 2:9ff.)? Was it typical for women to veil themselves or wear a particular hair style in the Greco-Roman world (see 1 Cor. 11:2–16)? And this raises another question: What was the place of women in the Greco-Roman world? All of these and other specific questions may be dealt with in the books listed above and in commentaries. On these questions, however, the best place to begin is by consulting Bible dictionaries and encyclopedias. Since Ferguson's book is so comprehensive, it is also quite helpful. The interpreter ought not to forget to consult other passages in the Bible that also touch on the specific issue under investigation. For example, if one were studying the "laying on of hands," it would be crucial to examine this practice in both the OT and NT.

These specific issues arise when one is interpreting a particular pericope, and thus this step should be listed in the steps given in the next part of the book. Nevertheless, for bibliographical purposes I decided to include this section here since it makes sense to keep the general and specific historical-cultural issues together.

Introductory Issues

Critical and introductory issues are examined so that the Pauline letters can be placed into their historical context. Here issues such as dating, authorship, and integrity come to the forefront. An important resource in this enterprise is the Book of Acts. Acts provides the reader with another perspective regarding the life and ministry of Paul. For example, Acts complements what the Epistles tell us about Paul's conversion and his Pharisaic background. Acts also supplies some background information about the inauguration of churches to which Paul wrote his letters. The interpreter should always read the Acts account of the founding of the church if Paul wrote an epistle to that community. Thus, the account of Paul's mission in Philippi (Acts 16:11–40) should be read

when one interprets Philippians. This same practice should
be followed in each letter if Acts records such an account.
Correlating the Pauline letters with Acts also provides crucial
information for the dating of the various letters.

We should mention that some scholars are averse to consulting Acts for reconstructing the history of the Pauline mission because they distrust its historical accuracy. A good case
can be made, however, for the historical veracity of Acts.[4] The
consultation of Acts is probably not essential for the interpretation of any of the letters. They stand on their own. We are
none the worse in the case of Colossians even though there is
no account of the founding of this church in Acts. Reading
Acts provides some help in placing the letters in chronological
order, and it also helps us understand Paul's movements more
precisely. The greatest value of Acts for the Pauline interpreter is the help it provides in establishing the history of the
early Pauline mission.

Before launching into the interpretation of a particular
passage or letter, the interpreter should read an introduction
of the letter under investigation. Introductions attempt to
answer the following questions: Who is the author? To whom
is the letter written? When was the letter written? Is the letter
a unity or is it a composite product of several letters? Does
the letter address any opponents, and, if so, can they be identified? Is the letter dependent upon other sources?

The value of studying introductory issues is that it assists
the student in interpreting a letter in its historical context.
Reading an introduction provides a brief summary and evaluation of the views of critical scholarship on the previously
mentioned questions. For example, one learns that seven of
the Pauline letters are accepted as authentic and genuinely
Pauline by nearly everyone: 1 Thessalonians, Galatians, 1–2
Corinthians, Romans, Philippians, and Philemon. Six of the
letters, however, are generally considered to be pseudony-

4. For a defense of basic historical accuracy, see W. W. Gasque, *A History of the
Criticism of the Acts of the Apostles* (Peabody, Mass.: Hendrickson, 1989); F. F. Bruce,
"The Acts of the Apostles To-day," *Bulletin of the John Rylands Library* 65 (1982): 35–56;
M. Hengel, *Acts and the History of Earliest Christianity* (Philadelphia: Fortress, 1979);
C. J. Hemer, "Luke the Historian," *Bulletin of the John Rylands Library* 60 (1977): 28–51;
A. N. Sherwin White, *Roman Society and Roman Law in the New Testament* (Grand
Rapids: Baker, 1978). Now see C. J. Hemer, *The Book of Acts in the Setting of Hellenistic
History*, ed. C. H. Gempf (Tübingen: J. C. B. Mohr, 1989).

mous: 2 Thessalonians, Colossians, Ephesians, 1–2 Timothy, and Titus. Clearly, one's view on the date and specific occasion of the letter will be bound up with one's conclusions regarding authorship, although dating the letters that are accepted as Pauline, such as Galatians and Philippians, can also be notoriously difficult.

I would recommend that students begin by reading the introductions by W. G. Kümmel and D. Guthrie on the particular letter in investigation. Kümmel is a moderately critical German scholar, and Guthrie is a British evangelical. From there one can consult other introductions (see end of this chapter), and articles on individual NT books in Bible dictionaries and encyclopedias. Also, the introductions at the beginning of major commentaries can be very valuable.

Consulting various introductions will acquaint the student with the major critical questions with respect to the Pauline epistles and show the student that different scholars hold diverse points of view on these critical questions. The student should note and evaluate the method and presuppositions of each scholar and summarize their major conclusions. Examination by the student of authors' methods and presuppositions should help the student understand why scholars reach different conclusions. Such careful analysis will also help the student make up his or her own mind about such questions.

The student should be aware that the conclusions of scholars on introductory issues are shaped by their interpretation of the letters. For example, all thirteen letters in the Pauline corpus claim to have been written by Paul. Some scholars believe that this attribution settles the question of authorship. However, other scholars doubt that all of these letters with the Pauline attribution are genuinely Pauline, since their interpretation of some of the letters points to inauthenticity. For example, the evidence from the Pastoral letters themselves makes it difficult to fit them into the life of Paul as portrayed in Acts. Moreover, some scholars claim that the theology of the Pastorals differs from the theology of the major Pauline letters. Also, the style of the Pastorals is clearly distinct from Paul's style in his other letters.

The point I am making here is that the views expressed in introductions regarding authorship, date, opponents, and unity always depend on the interpretation of the letter itself. By consulting the introduction the student receives a quick preview of how others have understood the letter. I emphasize this because students sometimes separate what they read in introductions from interpretation. There can be a tendency to view these books as repositories of unbiased, objective truth. Of course, much valuable and insightful information is contained in these books, but the student should evaluate what the introductions say by the evidence from the letter itself. Naturally this can be done more effectively after interpreting the entire letter. Reading the introduction at this early stage simply helps familiarize the interpreter with some of the major issues in the letter.

We cannot discuss all of the relevant introductory issues in detail here. However, we do want to touch very briefly on two issues, namely, integrity and authorship in the Pauline letters.

First, when we speak of the "integrity" of a letter we are asking whether that letter is a unified whole. Some scholars think that a number of Pauline letters, particularly Philippians and 2 Corinthians, are comprised of different letters that have been stitched together into a single composition by a later editor. For example, NT scholarship has commonly maintained that 2 Corinthians 10–13 is a separate letter that was written either before or after chapters 1–9, and a later editor placed chapters 10–13 after chapters 1–9. Obviously, such theories are quite complex and should be evaluated carefully. Two comments will be made here using 2 Corinthians as an example. First, even if 2 Corinthians is a composite letter, the task of the interpreter is to discuss the final redaction or edition of the Pauline letters. Of course, if chapters 10–13 were written later or earlier, such information would play a significant role when one reconstructs the history of Paul's relations with the Corinthians. But the first responsibility of the interpreter is to interpret the final form of the text. Second, there is no manuscript evidence that any part of 2 Corinthians was not an integral part of the letter from the beginning. Thus, the burden of proof is on the person who says that this letter (or any other Pauline letter) is not a unity. Indeed, it is possible (but unlikely in my view) that 2 Corinthians 10–13 was a letter written at a different point in time and under different circumstances. Ultimately, such issues must be determined by an exegesis of the documents themselves and by the weighing of historical and literary probabilities.[5]

Second, we will examine the issue of authorship, using the pastoral Epistles as our example since they are the first letters critics exclude from authenticity. On the one hand, it might seem to make very little difference whether or not Paul wrote the Pastorals. The interpreter would simply need to understand what the Pastorals are saying, and this could be achieved without knowing who the author is. The letter to the Hebrews can be understood even though we don't know the identity of the author. On the other hand, the issue of authorship becomes the crucial question for interpreting the Pastorals because one's decision regarding authenticity is directly linked with the historical situation that these letters address. The interpretation of some letters is not closely tied to the identity of the author (as we noted above in the case of Hebrews). And yet in the case of the Pastorals, the issues of interpretation, historical setting, and authorship are joined together so that one cannot neatly separate the argument of the letter from the historical situation that is being addressed. In other words, the interpretation of the Pastorals by commentators is controlled to some extent by decisions regarding their authorship and the historical circumstances surrounding the Pastorals.

We should add that a denial of the Pauline authorship of the Pastorals, for example, does not necessarily indicate a low view of Scripture. The argument can be made that pseudonymity was an accepted literary convention in the NT period.[6] A low view of the authority of Scripture is entailed

5. For a defense of the unity of 2 Corinthians, see P. E. Hughes, *Paul's Second Epistle to the Corinthians* (Grand Rapids: Eerdmans, 1962), xxi–xxxv. F. Young and D. F. Ford have provided a more recent defense in *Meaning and Truth in 2 Corinthians* (Grand Rapids: Eerdmans, 1987), 28–40.

6. For a defense of pseudonymity, see K. Aland, "The Problem of Anonymity and Pseudonymity in the Christian Literature of the First Two Centuries," *Journal of Theological Studies* 12 (1961): 39–49; D. G. Meade, *Pseudonymity and Canon: An Investigation into the Relationship of Authorship and Authority in Jewish and Earliest Christian Tradition* (Grand Rapids: Eerdmans, 1987). Meade did not really argue for pseudonymity but in large measure assumed it. For those who are still not persuaded that pseudonymity is found in the OT or the NT, such as the present author, Meade's book will not be persuasive. For a defense of authenticity, especially in epistolary literature, see D. Guthrie, *New Testament Introduction* (Downers Grove, Ill.: InterVarsity, 1970), 671–84.

only if one maintains that the Pastorals contradict other elements of Pauline theology (or the rest of Scripture). As we have already seen, one cannot live one's life based on Scripture if Scripture does not provide a coherent and consistent worldview. Even though pseudonymity is a theoretical possibility in the Pauline letters, I think that the evidence suggests that all thirteen letters are authentically Pauline. G. D. Fee, for instance, provided a cogent defense of the Pauline authorship of the Pastorals. In particular, Fee showed that Pauline authorship best explains the historical situation portrayed in the Pastorals, and that the theology of the Pastorals is in harmony with that of the previous Pauline Epistles.[7] Now if one accepts the Pastoral letters as authentic, then the other ten letters are most probably authentic as well, since the Pastorals are the first letters that are questioned regarding authenticity in Paul.

If one subscribes to the view that all thirteen letters are authentically Pauline, then all of the letters can be used to reconstruct Paul's theology. Those who have a more limited corpus for Paul are naturally hesitant about using the Pastorals and other letters they deem inauthentic when explicating Paul's theology.

Introductions and Surveys

> D. Guthrie, *New Testament Introduction*, 3d rev. ed. (Downers Grove, Ill.: InterVarsity, 1970 [revised edition forthcoming]). A massive and learned introduction from an evangelical perspective. Guthrie makes a persuasive case for the authenticity of all the Pauline letters.

> E. F. Harrison, *Introduction to the New Testament*, rev. ed. (Grand Rapids: Eerdmans, 1971). Similar to Guthrie but shorter and easier to read.

> W. G. Kümmel, *Introduction to the New Testament*, 17th ed. (Nashville: Abingdon, 1975). Standard German critical work.

> A. Wikenhauser, *New Testament Introduction* (New York: Herder, 1958). A helpful Roman Catholic introduction.

---

7. G. D. Fee, *1 and 2 Timothy, Titus* (Peabody, Mass.: Hendrickson, 1988), 1–31. The differences between some of the letters may also be due to the use of an amanuensis. See R. N. Longenecker, "Ancient Amanuenses and the Pauline Epistles," *New Dimensions in New Testament Study*, ed. R. N. Longenecker and M. C. Tenney (Grand Rapids: Zondervan, 1974), 281–97.

B. S. Childs, *The New Testament as Canon: An Introduction* (Philadelphia: Fortress, 1984). An insightful book that advances Childs' canonical approach.

L. T. Johnson, *The Writings of the New Testament: An Introduction* (Philadelphia: Fortress, 1986). An innovative and creative introduction focusing on the structure and content of the writings themselves, instead of on issues of authorship, date, and opponents.

R. H. Gundry, *A Survey of the New Testament*, rev. ed. (Grand Rapids: Zondervan, 1982). A very helpful survey for the beginning student.

G. W. Barker, W. L. Lane, and J. R. Michaels, *The New Testament Speaks* (New York: Harper & Row, 1969). A clearly written introduction and survey.

J. Drane, *Introducing the New Testament* (San Francisco: Harper & Row, 1986). A survey of the NT presented in an attractive way and a readable style.

B. M. Metzger, *The New Testament: Its Background, Growth and Content*, 2d enlarged ed. (Nashville: Abingdon, 1983). A useful introduction for the beginning student.

R. P. Martin, *New Testament Foundations: A Guide for Christian Students*, 2 vols. (Grand Rapids: Eerdmans, 1975, 1978). An innovative introduction.

C. F. D. Moule, *The Birth of the New Testament*, 3d ed. (New York: Harper & Row, 1982). A fresh approach.

J. A. T. Robinson, *Redating the New Testament* (Philadelphia: Westminster, 1976). In this creative work Robinson argued that all NT documents are to be dated previous to 70 A.D.

5

Diagramming and Conducting a Grammatical Analysis

I would like to relay my own experience with diagramming before explaining how one goes about doing it. I thought diagramming was superfluous when it was first assigned in one of my classes. Surely, the text could be understood without undergoing this tedious procedure. It is true that one *can* understand the Greek text without diagramming, but no one can comprehend the Greek text unless the grammar and syntax of the text are understood. And no one can claim to comprehend the syntax of the passage unless he or she is *able* to diagram the passage. Some people can understand a passage without diagramming it because they understand how every word and phrase relates in the sentence. This means, however, that they would be able to diagram the passage if they were asked to do so and knew the diagramming conventions. I began to see that diagramming forced me to think through the syntactical relationship of every word, phrase, and clause in the sentence. Diagramming compelled me to ask and answer questions that I would not always ask otherwise, such as, where does the participle go in this sentence, what kind of participle is this syntactically, and how does it relate to the rest of the sentence? And what word or words does the prepositional phrase modify?

One of the great values of diagramming, then, is that it

compels the interpreter to slow down and to think carefully through every element of the text, for the interpreter must make decisions about the placement of every word or phrase in the text. Diagramming is also helpful because it lays out the text visually. Such a schematic immediately shows the main clause, main verb, direct object(s), indirect object(s), modifiers, subordinate clauses (if any), and other key grammatical parts. Diagramming is particularly helpful in Pauline literature where the syntax is involved and complex, and the arguments tightly structured. By diagramming, one can unravel a Pauline text which initially appears to be a maze. For example, Ephesians 1:3–14 is one sentence in Greek. If an interpreter could not diagram this sentence, then the syntax of the sentence would not be clearly grasped. And if the interpreter does not understand a sentence syntactically, then he or she will lack confidence in the validity of his or her interpretation.

Diagramming is frightening to many people; for some it evokes horrible memories of the diagramming done in elementary school. My experience as a teacher, however, indicates that diagramming can be learned by anyone who is willing to work at it. Of course, it cannot be learned in a day. Most of my students are able to use diagramming as a useful tool after diagramming one passage per week for ten weeks. I have heard many comments from students who grow in confidence in their handling of the Greek as they diagram. Nothing can replace the first-hand analysis of the text that occurs when one diagrams. The challenge and excitement of unlocking the grammar of a text for oneself brings great satisfaction. This rigorous, grammatical analysis also better prepares the interpreter for evaluating the work of others in commentaries.

The following information is designed to give basic instructions in diagramming. Obviously, not every possible construction can be presented, but it is hoped that most of the main constructions are represented so that the student will have a good idea of how to proceed. Even though definite articles should technically be placed underneath the word they modify, I have put them on the same line so that the diagram does not become unnecessarily cluttered. There are different systems for diagramming, and I make no claim that *my* way is the *only* way to diagram.[1] My goal is to present as simple a system as possible. For the sake of simplicity, Greek accents and breathing marks are omitted in diagramming, and thus no accents or breathing marks are included in the examples below. Words implied by the Greek text are put in brackets.[2]

I should also say here that the following instructions on how to diagram assume the student knows the meaning of the terms used in Greek grammar. Thus, no attempt will be made to define terms such as predicate nominative, appositives, etc. The student who does not understand the terms should consult a beginning Greek grammar.

Specific Constructions

One should begin a diagram by locating the main verb, the subject and object of that verb (if it has one), and then the modifiers, subordinate clauses, etc.

1. The simple subject and its predicate verb are placed on a horizontal line. A vertical line that goes through the horizontal separates the subject and verb.

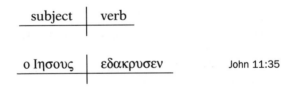

John 11:35

1. I have looked at a number of different sources and have borrowed from many, although I have not followed any one source consistently. I have used unpublished material that has been developed at Bethel Seminary over a number of years, but I am most indebted to the the unpublished notes from the Hermeneutics Syllabus of Daniel P. Fuller of Fuller Seminary (with his permission). He has carefully read this chapter and pointed out many defects, and thus I am grateful to him for making this chapter a better one. Nevertheless, I have not followed all of his suggestions, and any shortcomings in the chapter should be attributed to me. See also the following on diagramming: L. L. Kantenwein, *Diagrammatical Analysis*, rev. ed. (Winona Lake, Ind.: BMH Books, 1985); J. A. Brooks and C. L. Winbery, *Syntax of New Testament Greek* (Lanham, Md.: University Press, 1979), 139–47; W. S. LaSor, *Handbook of New Testament Greek: An Inductive Approach Based on the Greek Text of Acts* (Grand Rapids: Eerdmans, 1973), 2:137–44; S. McKnight, "New Testament Greek Grammatical Analysis," in *Introducing New Testament Interpretation*, ed. S. McKnight (Grand Rapids: Baker, 1989), 75–95.

2. One could also leave a blank space in places where words are implied, for usually the implied words are obvious from the context.

2. The direct object of a transitive verb follows the verb and is separated from it by a vertical line above the horizontal.

subject	verb	direct object

Μωυσης	υψωσεν	τον οφιν	John 3:14

3. Some verbs take two objects: one common construction is when there is an object of person (υμας) and an object of thing (παντα).

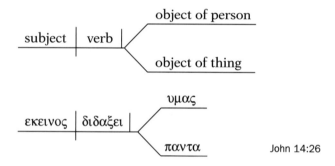

object of person

subject | verb

object of thing

υμας

εκεινος | διδαξει

παντα   John 14:26

4. Another construction with two objects is called the predicate accusative (or object complement). In this construction the second object completes the meaning of the first object. The predicate accusative follows the direct object with a line sloping toward the object to which it is related.

subject	verb	direct object \ predicate accusative

[αυτοι]	ειχον	Ιωαννην \ υπηρετην	Acts 13:5

5. A predicate nominative or predicate adjective is separated from the "to be" verb or another linking verb by a line that slopes back toward the subject to which it is related.

subject	copulative \ predicate nominative

| ο θεος | εστιν \ αγαπη | 1 John 4:8
|---|---|

6. An appositive is shown by the equal (=) sign.

appositive = subject	verb

| Παυλος = εγω | λεγω | Gal. 5:2
|---|---|

7. Words in the dative case (including indirect objects), without a preceding preposition, usually go under the main verb with a diagonal line.

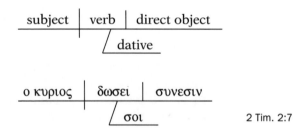

subject	verb	direct object

/ dative

ο κυριος	δωσει	συνεσιν

/ σοι   2 Tim. 2:7

8. Genitive modifiers go underneath the word they modify with a diagonal line.

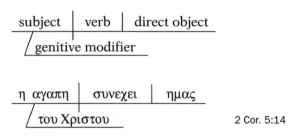

subject	verb	direct object

/ genitive modifier

η αγαπη	συνεχει	ημας

/ του Χριστου   2 Cor. 5:14

9. Some verbs take a genitive object or a dative object. These are portrayed in the same way as accusative direct objects.

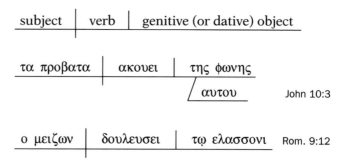

10. Prepositional phrases and adverbs go underneath the word they modify. Use a diagonal line for prepositional phrases. Adverbs can be put immediately under the verb without any line at all.

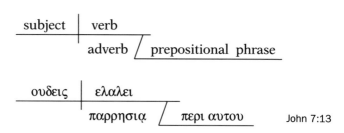

11. If a word or phrase does not modify the verb, and it modifies the first phrase which modifies the verb, then it is portrayed as follows:

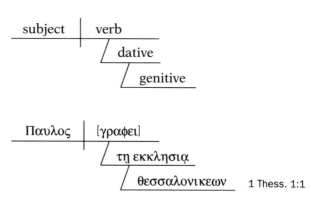

12. Attributive adjectives are placed underneath the word they modify with a diagonal line.

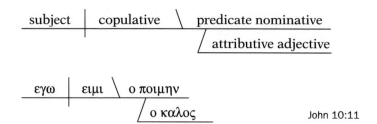

13. Periphrastics are diagrammed as follows:

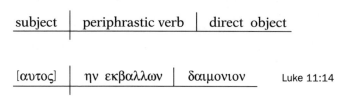

14. The following shows diagramming for constructions of two subjects and two verbs.

15. Vocatives and exclamations are disconnected from the main diagram lines.

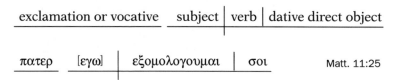

Only the word "πατερ" is in the vocative here.

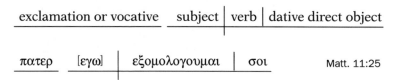

The word "αμην" is an exclamation here.

16. A relative clause is a subordinate clause, and it is placed
    underneath the main clause. A dashed line is drawn up
    to its antecedent.

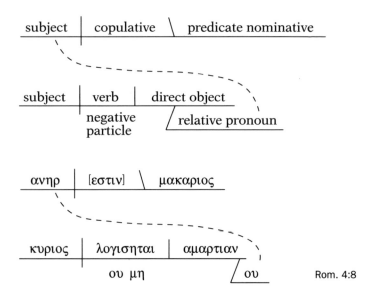

Rom. 4:8

17. An infinitive can be part of a subject clause. A subject
    clause is always put on stilts to identify it clearly as
    such.

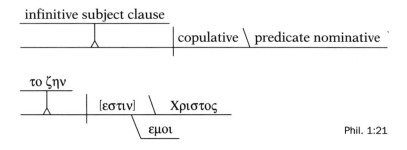

Phil. 1:21

18. Infinitives can function as part of an object clause, or as
    complementary infinitives with certain verbs.

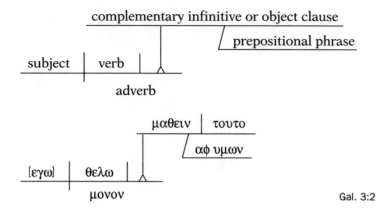

Gal. 3:2

It is difficult to distinguish between complementary infinitives and infinitives that are part of an object clause. Dan Fuller suggested to me that he has solved this problem by regarding infinitives that come off intransitive verbs as complementary, and infinitives that come off transitive verbs as part of an object clause.

19. Purpose, result, and temporal infinitives are placed underneath the main verb. Note in the example below that double lines separate the subject accusative (accusative of general reference) in the subordinate clause from the verb to which it is related.

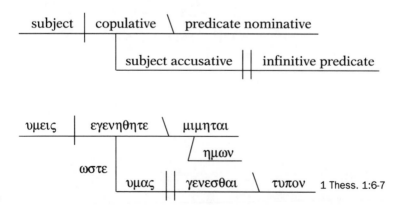

1 Thess. 1:6-7

20. An infinitive can modify another word just as adjectives or adverbs do.

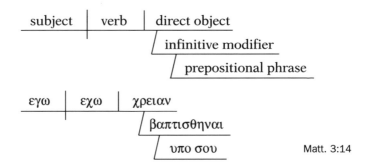

Matt. 3:14

21. A participle can function attributively. In this case it modifies the word just as an attributive adjective does. A diagonal line is used.

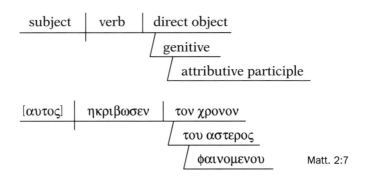

Matt. 2:7

22. A participle can also function substantively. In this case it functions as any other noun.

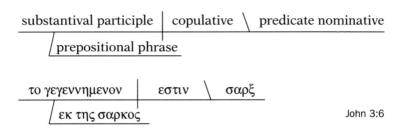

John 3:6

23. Adverbial participles (temporal, causal, conditional, etc.) are placed under the main verb with a vertical line.

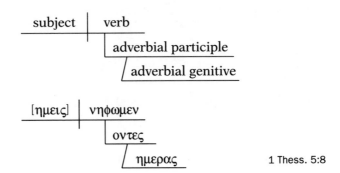

1 Thess. 5:8

24. A supplementary (complementary) participle follows the main verb.

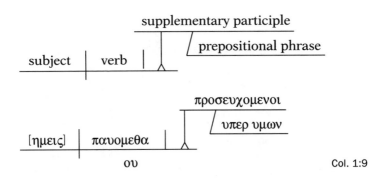

Col. 1:9

Supplementary participles can also follow a noun and still be linked to a verb.

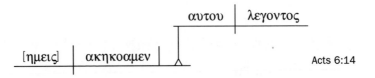

Acts 6:14

25. A genitive absolute construction is placed under the main verb, for all genitive absolutes are adverbial participles. A vertical dashed line is used to show that the construction is absolute.

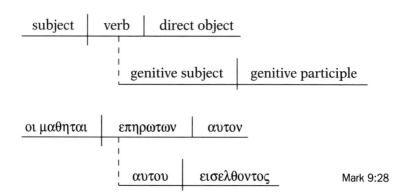

Mark 9:28

26. All subordinate clauses are placed under the main verb on diagonal lines: causal (ὅτι), result (ὥστε), purpose (ἵνα), temporal (ὅτε, ὅταν), locative (ὅπου), comparative (ὡς, καθώς), and conditional (εἰ, ἐάν).

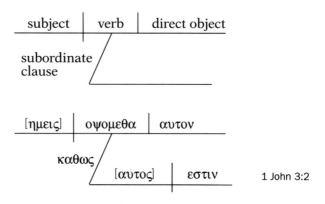

1 John 3:2

27. The words ὅτι and ἵνα can also be used to introduce subject or object clauses. In this case the clause is placed on stilts.

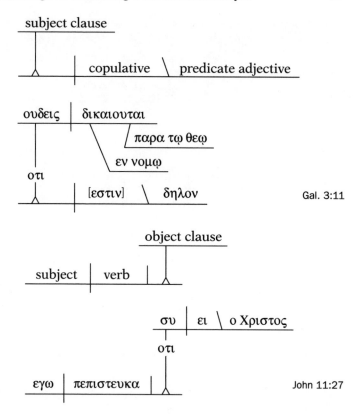

Gal. 3:11

John 11:27

28. Ἵνα and ὅτι may also further define a single word in a sentence. In this case they are explicative and diagrammed as follows:

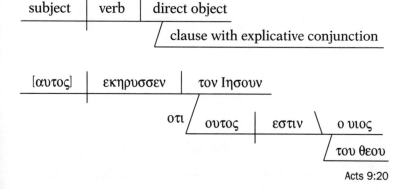

Acts 9:20

29. A μέν–δέ construction is diagrammed as follows:

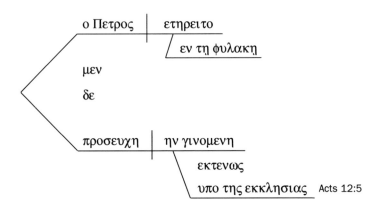

ο Πετρος | ετηρειτο

εν τη φυλακη

μεν

δε

προσευχη | ην γινομενη

εκτενως

υπο της εκκλησιας   Acts 12:5

30. Coordinating conjunctions indicate the beginning of a new independent clause, and thus should not be placed underneath the previous main verb. Instead they are placed above and before the main clause. The main coordinating conjunctions include ἀλλά, δέ, ἄρα, διό, γάρ, ἤ, καί (καί can also function as an adverb meaning "even" or "also"), μήδε, οὐδέ, οὔτε, οὖν, τέ, ὥστε.

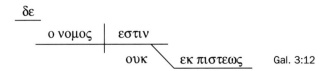

δε

ο νομος | εστιν

ουκ \ εκ πιστεως   Gal. 3:12

31. Subordinating conjunctions introduce dependent (subordinate) clauses and are placed under the main verb (see 26 above). Some of the most common subordinating conjunctions are ἐάν, εἰ, ἐπεί, ἵνα, καθώς, ὅπου, ὅπως, ὅταν, ὅτε, ὅτι, ὡς, ὥστε.

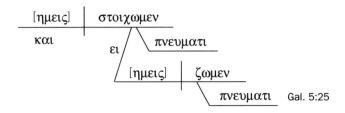

[ημεις] | στοιχωμεν

και

ει / πνευματι

[ημεις] | ζωμεν

πνευματι   Gal. 5:25

32. Questions are diagrammed as follows:

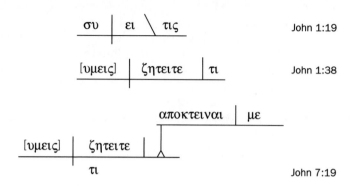

Here τί goes underneath the verb because it functions as an adverb.

33. A comparative that follows a preposition is portrayed as follows:

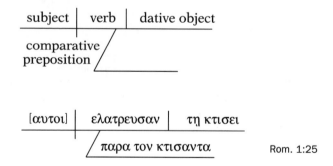

Final Note on Diagramming

I use vertical lines when an infinitive or participle functions adverbially, that is, when they modify a verb. If an infinitive or participle modifies a noun, adjective, or pronoun, then I use diagonal lines. Diagonal lines are used with all other constructions that are placed under the main clause except adverbs and negatives. Adverbs and negatives are placed immediately under the words they modify without any lines at all. One can slant diagonal lines either way. One may also use straight lines for modifiers. After all, the main issue is the accurate placement of the words, phrases, and clauses, not which way the lines slant.

The example below illustrates a comprehensive diagram of 1 Thessalonians 1:1–5.

1 Thess. 1:1

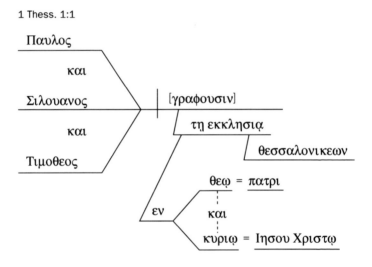

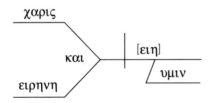

1:2

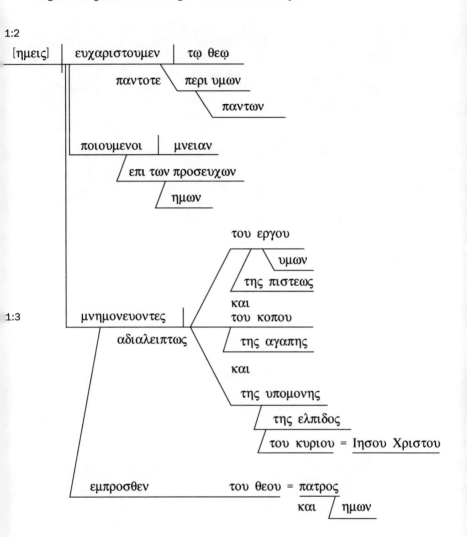

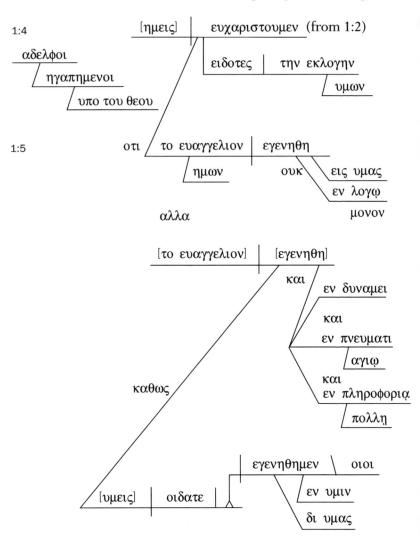

The Use of Grammars

The student can diagram only after identifying the syntactical function of every word. I usually pencil in next to the word or clause on the diagram the function of the word or clause being examined. Thus, next to an adverbial participle I might write: adverbial concessive.

The best way to learn grammar is by reading and diagramming the Greek text. Hands-on experience in doing interpretation is the ideal way to learn. I have also found that reading and studying grammars has sharpened my understanding of Greek. Some students find grammars daunting because they do not know how to use grammars as reference tools. All grammars, of course, have a table of contents. Most grammars, however, are also indexed. The advanced grammars contain a subject index (e.g., you may want to see what a grammarian says about objective genitives), a Scripture index, and an index of Greek words. The wise student will turn to these indexes often. The two sources immediately below are especially helpful for the beginner and both have useful bibliographies:

S. McKnight, "New Testament Greek Grammatical Analysis," in *Introducing New Testament Interpretation*, ed. S. McKnight (Grand Rapids: Baker, 1989), 75–95.

D. A. Carson, *Exegetical Fallacies* (Grand Rapids: Baker, 1984), 67–90.

Intermediate Grammars

J. A. Hewett, *New Testament Greek: A Beginning-Intermediate Grammar* (Peabody, Mass.: Hendrickson, 1986). A grammar that combines both beginning and intermediate Greek.

J. A. Brooks and C. L. Winbery, *Syntax of New Testament Greek* (Lanham, Md.: University Press, 1979). Probably the best intermediate grammar because it contains many helpful examples.

H. E. Dana and J. R. Mantey, *A Manual Grammar of the New Testament* (New York: Macmillan, 1927). Outdated but still useful.

J. H. Greenlee, *A Concise Exegetical Grammar of New Testament Greek*, 3d rev. ed. (Grand Rapids: Eerdmans, 1963). The word concise tells it all, for this book is very brief.

M. Zerwick, *Biblical Greek Illustrated by Examples* (Rome: Biblical Institute Press, 1963). A helpful tool since it is keyed to his *Grammatical Analysis of the Greek New Testament*.

A. T. Robertson and W. H. Davis, *A New Short Grammar of the Greek New Testament*, 10th ed. (New York: Harper & Brothers, 1933; Baker, 1977). A useful intermediate grammar for the student who is not ready to tackle Robertson's massive work (see below).

Advanced Tools

C. F. D. Moule, *An Idiom Book of New Testament Greek*, 2d ed. (Cambridge: Cambridge University Press, 1963). Clearly written with many helpful examples.

E. D. Burton, *Syntax of the Moods and Tenses in New Testament Greek*, 3d ed. (Chicago: University of Chicago Press, 1900; Grand Rapids: Kregel, 1976). An illuminating study of the Greek verb with many examples.

F. Blass and A. Debrunner, *A Greek Grammar of the New Testament and Other Early Christian Literature*, trans. and ed. R. W. Funk (Chicago: University of Chicago Press, 1961). This work is a mine of information. For the advanced student.

J. H. Moulton, W. F. Howard, and N. Turner, *A Grammar of New Testament Greek*, 4 vols. (Edinburgh: T. & T. Clark, 1906–1976). Volume III, *Syntax*, by Turner is particularly helpful for the student.

A. T. Robertson, *A Grammar of the Greek New Testament in the Light of Historical Research*, 4th ed. (Nashville: Broadman, 1934). A massive work of great value; dated in places and not well organized.

M. J. Harris, "Prepositions and Theology in the Greek New Testament," in *The New International Dictionary of New Testament Theology*, ed. C. Brown (Grand Rapids: Zondervan, 1978) 3:1171–1215. A valuable article that includes many exegetical examples.

6

Tracing the Argument

One of the most challenging parts of the exegetical process is the reconstruction of the argument used by Paul. In this step the interpreter asks questions about the function of different propositions in the text until he or she can see how the entire paragraph or letter fits together. In the case of Pauline literature, the interpreter must examine Paul's carefully crafted arguments in order to unfold his message to specific churches with specific needs. The interpreter who endeavors to do this will undoubtedly acquire more confidence in doing exegesis, knowing that he or she can piece together the structure of a passage and explain the structure to others.

In the last chapter we explained in some detail how to diagram. No one can follow the thread of Paul's arguments if the syntax and grammar of the text are not understood. If one cannot diagram a Pauline text, then one will have difficulty in tracing the argument of that text. The ability to diagram the text and the ability to follow an argument go hand in hand.

I am convinced that tracing the structure of the argument in the Pauline epistles is the most important step in the exegetical process. One of the weaknesses in many commentaries today is the failure to trace the argument in each paragraph, and the failure to explain how each paragraph relates to preceding and following paragraphs.[1] Instead, the commentaries focus on individual words and verses. Readers gain

1. For this same criticism, see P. Cotterell and M. Turner, *Linguistics and Biblical Interpretation* (Downers Grove, Ill.: InterVarsity, 1989), 223–25. For an exception to this, see C. Caragounis (*The Ephesian "Mysterion": Meaning and Content* [Lund: Gleerup,

much knowledge about individual elements of the text, but they do not acquire an understanding of the argument of each paragraph or of the complete text.

The student should understand from the beginning that this step involves effort and discipline. Not only should the student know Greek and be able to diagram, but he or she must also discover the function of every proposition in a Pauline letter. Hard thinking like this cannot be achieved if one does not avoid distractions (like the radio or television) when studying. So where does the student turn to find a method that will help him or her to reconstruct the line of reasoning in a Pauline text? The best method I have found is presented by Daniel P. Fuller in his as yet unpublished work on hermeneutics. I am heavily dependent on Fuller in the following exposition of this method.[2]

Propositions

The key to tracing the argument in the Pauline letters is by understanding the relationship between different proposi-

---

1977]), who presents his understanding of the structure of some texts in Ephesians. A careful analysis of the structure of the text is also apparent in the exegesis of Romans 9:1–23 by John Piper in *The Justification of God: An Exegetical and Theological Study of Romans 9:1–23* (Grand Rapids: Baker, 1983). Piper was a student of Dan Fuller's. Contemporary commentaries often show a careful analysis of the structure of the text, but perhaps the structure is not being set forth in a manner that is explicit enough for students. Older commentaries were often more successful in communicating the structure. See, for example, C. Hodge, *Commentary on the Epistle to the Romans*, rev. ed. (New York: Armstrong and Son, 1900).

2. This material is included with Fuller's permission. Fuller's categories for the propositions, his definitions, and many of his specific examples are used here. There are some adaptations where I have combined different categories together or changed the wording for some definitions. Nevertheless, the substance of this chapter is found in Fuller. If he publishes his valuable work on hermeneutics, the reader can compare this chapter to Fuller's work and clearly see how much I stand in his debt for this chapter. I am also grateful to Dan Fuller for reading this chapter (although I should note that he did not read the three examples at the end of the chapter). He pointed out a number of deficiencies and made many helpful suggestions that have improved it. Nevertheless, he is not in agreement with several elements in this chapter. Thus, any weaknesses here should be attributed to me rather than to Fuller. I have also consulted and used some of the material in the book by J. Beekman and J. Callow, *Translating the Word of God* (Grand Rapids: Zondervan, 1974); see especially pp. 287–312, although all of 267–342 is relevant. See also E. A. Nida, J. P. Louw, A. H. Snyman, J. v. W. Cronje, *Style and Discourse* (Capetown: Bible Society, 1983), 99–144; Cotterell and Turner, *Linguistics and Biblical Interpretation*, 188–229; J. P. Louw, *Semantics of New Testament Greek* (Philadelphia: Fortress, 1982), 67–158.

tions in the text. Paul did not usually write proverbially, offering random bits of advice to his congregations. He usually engaged in a sustained argument in his letters. We cannot understand his arguments unless we can set forth and trace the building blocks of his reasoning. The building blocks of his reasoning are found in his propositions. Thus, if the thread of Paul's line of reasoning is to be discerned, we must understand the relationship between different propositions. In this chapter we shall explain and classify the different kinds of propositions, and then give some examples of how to trace the argument in the Pauline letters.

What is a proposition? A proposition is an assertion or statement about something. The words "she ate" is a proposition, for it makes a statement or an assertion about something. In order to be a proposition, a statement must have a subject and predicate. The subject or predicate can be implied. If my child were to run toward the street I would yell, "Stop!" The one word "stop" is a proposition because the implied subject is "you," and the imperative verb "stop" is the predicate.

Relationships Between Propositions

How do propositions relate to one another? All propositions relate in either a *coordinate* or *subordinate* way to previous propositions. We can see the relation between propositions in sentences. For instance, coordinate propositions are found in compound sentences. Compound sentences have two or more independent clauses joined together. The sentence "I listened to the radio, and I washed my car" is a compound sentence. Both of these clauses are independent and could be separate sentences. Also, there is no dependent relationship between the two clauses. Two separate activities were performed: washing the car and listening to the radio. However, these two clauses can easily be rewritten so that one clause is a *subordinate* clause. If I write, "I listened to the radio while I washed my car," then the sentence is now a complex sentence (containing at least one subordinate clause) instead of a compound sentence. The clause "while I washed my car" is not an independent clause but a subordinate one. In fact, it is a temporal subordinate clause because it explains *when* I listened to the radio. The independent clause "I listened to the radio" is a sentence in its own right, but the clause "while I washed the car" is not a sentence. The latter clause is dependent (subordinate) upon the main clause in the sentence; it indicates *when* I listened to the radio.

We should note that coordinate and subordinate relations do not exist only in individual sentences. A paragraph or a larger section in a work may be coordinate or subordinate to another paragraph or larger section. Thus, when we say that a proposition is subordinate, we are not always referring to a subordinate clause in an individual sentence. A sentence, paragraph, or larger section may be subordinate conceptually to another sentence, paragraph, or larger section without being a subordinate clause in a sentence. In other words, a proposition may be subordinate conceptually without being subordinate grammatically. Generally speaking, it is easier to see the relations within sentences than the relations between two different paragraphs.

Coordinate Relationships

We will examine the three different kinds of coordinate relationships: *series, progression*, and *alternative*. As we delineate the different kinds of propositions, each category will be briefly defined. In addition, common conjunctions that are used for each category will be listed both in English and Greek. The listing of these conjunctions is not exhaustive; some of the most common are listed. Also, we will offer examples from the NT for each category.

1. *Series*. The relationship between propositions is a series when each proposition makes its own independent contribution to the whole. The following illustrates this: "She laughed, and she sang." Both propositions make an independent statement, and neither is dependent on the other in any way. Nor is there any sense of attaining a climax in this sentence. Propositions in a series may refer to several events that occur at the same time or may also portray events that occur chronologically.

   Conjunctions: and, moreover, furthermore, likewise, neither . . . nor (καί, δέ, τέ, οὔτε, οὐδέ, μήτε, μηδέ)
   Examples: "The sun will be darkened, *and* the moon

will not give its light, *and* the stars will fall from the sky, *and* the heavenly bodies will be shaken" (Matt. 24:29). "Be joyful in hope, patient in affliction, faithful in prayer" (Rom. 12:12). (Note that this last example lacks the word "and," but it is clearly a series.)

2. **Progression**. The relationship between propositions is called progression when each proposition is a step closer toward a climax. The statement, "Jesus became a man, and he lived humbly, and he died a criminal's death," is clearly an example of progression. Even though Jesus became a man, he could have lived as a king. And even though he lived humbly, he could have died a noble death. Thus each proposition builds toward a climax and serves to show the extent of his love.

   Conjunctions: then, and, moreover, furthermore, neither . . . nor (καί, δέ, τέ, οὔτε, οὐδέ, μήτε, μηδέ)
   Examples: "And those he predestined, he also called; *and* those whom he called he also justified; *and* those whom he justified he also glorified" (Rom. 8:30). "The earth produces of itself, *first* the blade, *then* the ear, *then* the full grain in the ear" (Mark 4:28).

3. **Alternative**. Each proposition expresses different possibilities arising from a situation. For example, consider the following: "I could work on this book, or I could watch the tennis match on television." Here I have two alternatives for how I spend my time.

   Conjunctions: or, but, while, on the one hand . . . on the other hand (ἀλλά, δέ, ἤ, μέν . . . δέ)
   Examples: "Some were convinced by what he said, *while* others disbelieved" (Acts 28:24). "Are you he who is to come, *or* shall we look for another?" (Matt. 11:3).

Subordinate Relationships

Subordinate propositions are those that do not stand alone but are related in some supporting way to the main proposition. Subordinate propositions can be divided into three different types: those that support by *restatement*, those that support by *distinct statement*, and those that support by *contrary statement*.

The student should note that there are nine different kinds of adverbial clauses in the categories listed below. Not all of the categories contain adverbial clauses, but the student's ability to identify propositions will be strengthened if the nine different types of adverbial clauses are mastered. The nine types that appear in the subordinate clauses below are: (1) modal, (2) comparative, (3) causal, (4) result, (5) conditional, (6) purpose, (7) temporal, (8) locative, and (9) concessive. These will be highlighted in each category so that the student can begin to master these types of subordinate clauses.

Support by Restatement

The main proposition may be supported by restatement, that is, by further defining or explaining the main proposition. There are five ways by which this can be accomplished. A list of these different kinds of restatement clauses with NT examples follows.

1. ***Action-Manner***. The statement of an action, and then a more precise statement that indicates the way or manner in which this action is carried out. For example, "Last night I cleaned my house by vacuuming the carpet and dusting the furniture." Vacuuming and dusting explain in more precise detail how I cleaned the house. Used in *modal clauses*.

   Key words: by, in that
   Examples: "He emptied himself *by* taking the form of a servant" (Phil 2:7). "She brought much gain to her masters *by* prophesying" (Acts 16:16).

2. ***Comparison***. A statement or action in the main proposition is explained more precisely by a comparative statement showing what the statement in the main proposition is like. For instance, if someone says, "I love you like a brother," the phrase "like a brother" further describes the kind of love that one has. Used in *comparative clauses*.

   Conjunctions: just as, even as, like, as . . . so (ὡς, καθώς, οὕτως, ὥσπερ)
   Examples: "Be imitators of me, *just as* I also am of Christ" (1 Cor. 11:1). "*As* the Father has sent me, *so* send I you" (John 20:21).

3. **Negative-Positive**. Two alternatives are given: one is denied and the other is affirmed. The sentence, "It is not hot, but it is cold" explains in more detail what the writer means in saying that it is not hot. The antithetical statement explains that it is the opposite of hot, that is, it is cold. Note that the order of these can be reversed so that the positive precedes the negative. The two statements may be essentially synonymous (first example below), or they may stand in contrast (second example below).

Particles and conjunctions: not, but (οὐ, μή, ἀλλά, δέ)
Examples: "Do *not* be foolish, *but* understand what the will of the Lord is" (Eph 5:17). "We are fools for the sake of Christ, *but* you are wise in Christ" (1 Cor. 4:10).

4. **Idea-Explanation**. The addition of a clarifying statement to the main proposition is also considered an example of support by restatement. For example, "There is a drought, that is, there has been no rain for three months." Here we have an idea and an explanation that further explicates the idea. The clarifying statement either explains the whole of the preceding statement (first example below), or one word of the preceding statement (second example below).

Conjunctions: that is, for (τοῦτ' ἔστιν, γάρ)
Examples: "Jacob supplanted me these two times; he took away my birthright and now he has taken away my blessing" (Gen 27:36). "And they drank of the rock that followed them, and the rock was Christ" (1 Cor. 10:4).

5. **Question-Answer**. The question is stated and the answer to the question is given. The question and answer (the answer is implied if the question is rhetorical) can often be rephrased as a statement.

Examples: "Shall we continue in sin in order that grace might increase? May it never be!" (Rom. 6:1). "What does the Scripture say? Abraham believed God . . ." (Rom. 4:3). The latter could be rephrased as, "Scripture says that Abraham believed God."

Support by Distinct Statement

Subordinate propositions that support by distinct statement allow the author to develop his point further. Eight different categories are found within this second group of subordinate propositions. We now proceed to give definitions and NT examples for these eight categories of subordinate relationships that support by distinct statement.

1. **Ground**. A statement is made in the main proposition, and the subordinate one gives a reason or ground for the statement. "Do not eat the berries because they are poisonous." The word *because* introduces the clause that provides the ground or reason for the command not to eat the berries. In this case the supporting proposition always follows the main one. We should note here that the word "for" (γάρ) can also introduce Idea-Explanation. This little word is extremely important and requires careful interpretation. Used in *causal clauses*.

   Conjunctions: for, because, since (γάρ, ὅτι, ἐπεί, ἐπειδή, διότι)

   Examples: "Blessed are the poor in spirit, *for* theirs is the kingdom of heaven" (Matt. 5:3). "If they do not have self control, let them marry, *for* it is better to marry than to burn" (1 Cor. 7:9).

2. **Inference**. A statement or event from which a conclusion or inference is drawn. The only difference from the previous category is that the supporting proposition precedes. One should note here that inference and ground function similarly. The difference between them is the order of their propositions. If a proposition is a ground, then the supporting statement comes *after* the statement it supports. For example, "I worship Jesus *because he is God*." If an inference is being drawn, then the support for that inference is found in the first proposition. Thus, the same sentence would appear as follows if the second proposition draws an inference from the first: "Jesus is God, *therefore, I worship him*."

   Conjunctions: therefore, wherefore, consequently, accordingly (οὖν, διό, ὥστε)

Examples: "The end of all things is at hand, *therefore*, be sensible and sober for prayer" (1 Pet 4:7). "Consider yourselves dead to sin and alive to God in Christ Jesus. *Therefore*, do not let sin reign in your mortal body . . . " (Rom. 6:11–12).

3. *Action-Result*. The relationship between an action and a consequence or result that accompanies that action. "It did not rain for three months, so there was a drought." The drought resulted directly from the lack of rain. Used in *result clauses*.

   Conjunctions: so that, that, with the result that (ὥστε)
   Examples: "There arose a great storm in the sea, *so that* the boat was being swamped by the waves" (Matt. 8:24). "God so loved the world *that* he gave his only begotten Son" (John 3:16).

4. *Action-Purpose*. An action-purpose proposition involves an action to accomplish a certain outcome. "He quit eating desserts so that he could lose weight." Notice that Action-Result and Action-Purpose are very close in meaning. The difference is that Action-Purpose focuses on *an intended result* which may not come to fruition. In the example above the person who stopped eating desserts purposed and intended to lose weight, but he may not lose any. Sometimes it is exegetically difficult to decide whether a clause is purpose or result. Used in *purpose clauses*.

   Conjunctions: in order that, that, with a view to, to the end that, lest (ἵνα, ὅπως, ἵνα . . . μή)
   Examples: "I long to see you, *that* I might impart some spiritual gift to strengthen you" (Rom. 1:11). "For good reason do you reject the command of God *in order that* you might establish your own tradition" (Mark 7:9).

5. *Conditional*. Conditional propositions show that the causing action is potential only. "If she scores 95 on her exam, then she will earn an 'A' in the class." The 'A' is not guaranteed, but conditioned on her getting a 95. The

result will be obtained only if the condition is met. We should note, however, that with some conditional clauses in the NT, the context clearly indicates that the stated condition is a reality. For example, "If we have died with Christ, we believe that we shall also live together with him" (Rom. 6:8). It is evident from the context that Paul believes that it is true that Christians have died with Christ, and so it follows that believers will also live with him. In cases where the condition is an assumed reality, the conditional clause is really equivalent to a ground. Used in *conditional clauses*.

Conjunctions: if . . . then, if, provided that, except (εἰ, ἐάν)

Examples: "*If* you are led by the Spirit, you are not under law" (Gal. 5:18). "*If* any person is overtaken in any trespass, you the spiritual ones should restore such a one in a spirit of gentleness" (Gal. 6:1).

6. ***Temporal.*** The relationship between the main proposition and the occasion when it occurs. Temporal propositions describe the time period in which the action in the main proposition is carried out. In the sentence "Jim ate a candy bar after he went to the store," the temporal clause tells us that the candy bar was eaten subsequent to going to the store. Even though temporal clauses focus on the time of a particular action, a causal idea may be implicit. The sentence "After I cleaned up my room, I received my allowance," stresses the time relation between the two clauses, but it is also possible that the author is implicitly suggesting that the allowance was received *because* the room was cleaned. Nevertheless, the presence of a temporal clause demonstrates that the author desired to emphasize the occasion rather than the cause of the action described in the independent clause. Used in *temporal clauses*.

Conjunctions: when, whenever, after, before (ὅτε, ὅταν)
Examples: "*When* you fast, do not look gloomy" (Matt. 6:16). "Count it all joy, my brothers, *whenever* you encounter various trials" (James 1:2).

7. **Locative.** Locative propositions indicate the place in which the action occurred, or the place where the action is operative. Consider the following: "Where one sees vultures, one will find a dead body." The locative clause informs us where vultures will be, namely, near a corpse. Locative clauses, like temporal ones, can also have an implicit causal idea. For example, Ruth said to Naomi, "Whither you go, I will go" (Ruth 1:16). This is a locative clause, but it is also clear that Ruth will go *because* Naomi goes. Used in *locative clauses*.

> *Key words*: where, wherever (ὅπου, οὗ)
> *Examples*: "*Where* two or three are gathered together in my name, there I am in their midst" (Matt. 18:20). "*Where* the Spirit of the Lord is, there is liberty" (2 Cor. 3:17).

8. **Bilateral.** A bilateral proposition supports two other propositions: one preceding and one following. This is not really a new category. It is simply an example of a proposition that is the ground of the preceding proposition, and an inference is drawn from it in the subsequent proposition. Examine the following: "May God be praised. He is good. Praise him forever." In this simple example the statement "He is good" functions as the ground for the first statement, "May God be praised." In addition, an inference is drawn from his goodness, namely, that he should be praised forever.

> *Conjunctions*: See numbers 1 and 2 above.
> *Example*: Only one example will be given here since these are inevitably longer. "*For* when you judge others you condemn yourself as well, *for* you the one judging do the same things, *therefore*, we know that God's judgment is according to the truth upon those who practice such things (Rom. 2:1b–2).

Support by Contrary Statement

In subordinate relationships the main proposition may also be supported by contrary statement. For those propositions that fit this type of subordinate relationship, there are two categories of subordinate propositions.

1. **Concessive.** A concessive proposition develops the argument with a contrary statement that contrasts the main proposition with the concessive one. Consider the following: "Even though he was only five feet tall, he could stuff a basketball." Here the main clause is supported by the concessive clause. The concessive clause indicates that the proposition in the main clause stands, even though there are conditions that would cause one to expect the opposite. No one expects a five foot person to stuff a basketball, and thus it is all the more remarkable when he can. Used in *concessive clauses*.

   Conjunctions: although . . . yet, although, yet, nevertheless, but (καίπερ, εἰ, καί, ἐάν καί). We should note here that the conjunction "but" is ambiguous. It may occur in alternative propositions, negative-positive propositions, or concessive ones.

   Examples: "*Although* he was a Son, he learned obedience from what he suffered" (Heb. 5:8). "*Though* you have 10,000 instructors in Christ, *yet* you do not have many fathers" (1 Cor. 4:15).

2. **Situation-Response.** Situation-Response is the relationship between a situation in one proposition and a response in another. Depending upon the person's response, the relationship between the two statements can be either positive or negative. However, Situation-Response differs from Action-Result. In Action-Result the effect is usually an inevitable result of the described action, whereas Situation-Response focuses on a person's response. Depending upon the person's response, the relationship between the two statements can be either positive or negative. In the examples listed below, the first illustrates a negative response, the second, a positive.

   Examples: "How often I would have gathered your children together as a hen gathers her brood under her wings, and you would not" (Matt. 23:38). "Jesus did this beginning of signs . . . , and his disciples believed in him" (John 2:11).

Further Comments on Propositions

The student should master the nine different kinds of adverbial clauses that we highlighted above. As we have seen, these propositions can be introduced by various conjunctions. However, these propositions can also be introduced by adverbial participles. Adverbial participles can be modal, causal, conditional, temporal, concessive, or show purpose. Adverbial infinitives may also introduce subordinate clauses, which can be temporal, causal, resultative, or show purpose. The student should study and master the helpful examples of these categories in Brooks-Winbery.[3] The student should retranslate subordinate clauses with a subject and a finite verb and specify in the translation the relationship between the main clause and the subordinate clause. For example, Romans 5:1 literally reads, "Having been justified by faith, we have peace with God." This is clearly a causal participle and it should be translated as follows: "Because we have been justified by faith, we have peace with God." Another example occurs in Acts 5:30, which says, "You killed him hanging him on a tree." It should be retranslated, "You killed him in that you hanged him on a tree." In other words, the student should not translate the second proposition "hanging him on a tree," nor should it even be rendered "by hanging him on a tree." Instead, the subject should be explicitly included so that the clause is translated "in that *you hanged* him on a tree." Note that by supplying an explicit subject the participle "hanging" is now rendered in translation as the finite verb "hanged."

Students often have questions about prepositional phrases and relative clauses. Normally I do not introduce a new proposition when relative clauses or prepositions are used. For instance, "Jim, who was a weaver, went to the store" contains the relative clause "who was a weaver." One could split this into two propositions: "Jim went to the store" would be the idea and "who was a weaver" would be the explanation. Even though the relative clause could be analyzed this way, I usually do not make a new proposition with the relative

3. J. A. Brooks and C. L Winbery, *Syntax of New Testament Greek* (New York: University Press, 1979), 120–24, 132–38. Note that Brooks and Winbery distinguished between modal and instrumental participles, whereas all instrumental and modal participles fall under the Action-Manner category in the system explained in this chapter.

clause unless I deem the relative clause to be particularly significant exegetically. For instance, Romans 6:2 literally reads, "We who have died to sin, how shall we still live in it?" The relative clause here is "we who have died to sin." I think it is justified to identify a discrete proposition in the relative clause here because the relative clause is the foundation of Paul's entire argument. In other words, Paul is saying: "We should not live in sin any more *because* we have died to sin." The relative clause ("we who have died to sin") actually provides the ground for the claim that we should not live in sin.

The advice given for relative clauses above also applies to attributive participles. Attributive participles, which modify another substantive, should not usually be set off as new propositions. For example, in Philippians 4:7 Paul says, "The peace of God which passes all understanding shall guard your hearts and minds in Christ Jesus." Now the word ὑπερέχουσα ("which passes") in this verse modifies εἰρήνη ("peace"), and the participle here is attributive. No new proposition is introduced by the words "which passes," and thus one should not split this sentence into two propositions.

Prepositional phrases do not add a new proposition to a sentence. In the sentence "Jill ate her sandwich in the house," the words "in the house" are a prepositional phrase, but they do not constitute a new proposition. These words are part of the single proposition stated in the sentence. Nevertheless, on some occasions the prepositional phrase may seem so significant exegetically that a new proposition is demanded. For instance, in Ephesians 1:6–14 Paul used a prepositional phrase three times, indicating the reason why God has showered the church with every spiritual blessing in Christ. He did this "for the praise of the glory of his grace" (1:6, εἰς ἔπαινον δόξης τῆς χάριτος αὐτοῦ), "for the praise of his glory" (1:12, εἰς ἔπαινον δόξης αὐτοῦ), "for the praise of his glory" (1:14, εἰς ἔπαινον τῆς δόξης αὐτοῦ). Note that all three of these constructions begin with the same preposition in Greek. Usually such prepositional phrases should not be made a separate proposition. But the threefold repetition of this phrase, and its obvious significance in context signals to the reader that discrete propositions are warranted for these prepositional phrases.[4]

4. Louw (*Semantics*, 82–83) rightly noted that prepositional phrases if unpacked may be retranslated so that they express a clause.

In summary. prepositional phrases, attributive participles, and relative clauses will normally not be separated into new propositions. On some occasions, however, the content of these constructions will be significant enough so that separation into new propositions is warranted. Of course, this means that on some occasions different interpreters will disagree on whether a relative clause or a prepositional phrase is exegetically significant enough to be made into a new proposition.

Sentences with direct and indirect discourse can be baffling to the student. An example is found in the sentence "I have believed that Jesus is the Christ." This sentence contains only one proposition, and that proposition really begins with the word "that." The words "I have believed" simply introduce the source of the proposition. All verbs of mental and physical perception, such as "think," "know," "see," "consider," and "realize," should be handled in the same way. These words do not contain a separate proposition per se; the clauses which stand as the objects of these verbs of perception contain the actual substance of the propositions.

A one sheet summary of the different relationships will be helpful so that the student can quickly scan the various categories. The abbreviation for each category is in the parentheses.

    I. Coordinate Relationships
      A. Series (S)
      B. Progression (P)
      C. Alternative (A)
    II. Subordinate Relationships
      A. Support by Restatement
        1. Action-Manner (Ac/Mn)
        2. Comparison (Cf)
        3. Negative-Positive (–/+)
        4. Idea-Explanation (Id/Exp)
        5. Question-Answer (Q/A)
      B. Support by Distinct Statement
        1. Ground (G)
        2. Inference (∴)
        3. Action-Result (Ac/Res)
        4. Action-Purpose (Ac/Pur)

      5. Conditional (If/Th)
      6. Temporal (T)
      7. Locative (L)
      8. Bilateral (BL)
   C. Support by Contrary Statement
      1. Concessive (Csv)
      2. Situation-Response (Sit/R)

Some Final Comments on the Method

Before we proceed on to some examples on how to relate the various propositions in Paul, a few comments should be made about the method itself. We should remember that the identification of the different relations between propositions reflects an exegetical judgment, an exegetical conclusion about the passage. For example, whether one sees propositions as reflecting a series or progression is an interpretive judgment. Nevertheless, the context usually contains clues that suggest that one category is right rather than another. Incorrect interpretations run aground on some trait in the text that does not yield the meaning suggested by the flawed interpretation. Correct interpretations explain satisfactorily every trait in the text.

One concern I have heard raised about the method is that not all Pauline texts are written in such a logical way. This is a helpful caution, for it warns us against imposing an alien structure on any Pauline text. It may be that Paul did not always present his case in a logical fashion. The interpreter should let the text unfold itself in a distinctive way and not force a pattern onto the text. Nevertheless, this method does not assume that all Pauline texts are logically structured. This method can account for texts that simply contain random observations. In such a case there would simply be a series of propositions that do not build upon one another in any discernible way. I have found, however, that Paul usually builds his argument from section to section so that you can discern a connected structure. Of course, Paul did not write in logical syllogisms in which every premise of his argument is carefully set forth, and then a conclusion is drawn from the premise(s). He often skips steps in his argument.

Finally, different interpreters will surely disagree on the

structure of different passages. We hope that such disagreement will impel all to return to the text again in order to see what Paul really said. The reader should also note that this method is not the whole of the exegetical process. What Cotterell and Turner said about their method of portraying the text is true of this method as well: "The model is not the structure, but our emerging hypothesis about it. The model does not provide us with *new information* but may be expected to give us an *overall perspective* of the structure when we have examined the relations of the individual pieces."[5]

Using the Method

Tracing the argument involves three steps: (1) isolate the different propositions; (2) trace the argument schematically; and (3) explain the main and supporting points in the text. I suggest that students trace the arguments in paragraphs.[6] The ultimate goal in the Pauline letters is to trace the argument in each paragraph, and then trace the argument between all the paragraphs so that the structure of the entire letter is evident. The best way to learn how to do this, as with any skill, is to practice it. Since this area is so crucial for exegesis, it is necessary to offer several examples so that the student will know how to proceed.

Example #1

Our first example is from 1 Timothy 6:1–2.[7] First, the student must isolate the different propositions in the passage. Every proposition should be translated with a subject and predicate. The translation should also reflect the relationship between the propositions. A conjunction or particle describing the relation should be supplied if there is not one. I put these key linking words in italics. The translation below reflects the propositions in 1 Timothy 6:1–2. Propositions that support other propositions are indented so that the reader

5. Cotterell and Turner, *Linguistics and Biblical Interpretation*, 196.

6. See Louw, *Semantics*, vii, 127–28. He pointed out that traditional methods of delineating paragraphs can be helpful, although one cannot determine where one paragraph ends and another begins until one has analyzed the text.

7. All of the possible interpretive issues in this text cannot be examined here. For a more detailed defense of the interpretation suggested here, see G. D. Fee, *1 and 2 Timothy, Titus* (Peabody, Mass.: Hendrickson, 1988), 137–39.

can see the main proposition(s) and can see which propositions support the main one. Main propositions are not indented in the paragraph.

> 1a Those under the yoke of slavery should consider their
> own masters worthy of all honor
>> 1b *in order that* the name of God should not be
>> spoken against
>> 1c *and in order that* the teaching should not be
>> spoken against
> 2a *That is*, those slaves who have believing masters
> should not despise them
>> 2b *because* they are brothers
> 2c *but instead*, they should serve their believing
> masters
>> 2d *because* those benefiting from the good work are
>> believers and beloved

Second, the interpreter must trace the relationships between the different propositions. The interpreter has made some of these decisions in the translation, but a more comprehensive analysis of the text is still needed. Brackets are placed next to the propositions so that the interpreter can portray the text in a schematic way and thereby see clearly how the text has been analyzed. The brackets closest in reflect the most minute analysis of the text, while the farthest bracket represents the most comprehensive analysis of the text. The relationship between the different propositions should be written down in the brackets. The abbreviations given above should be used. First Timothy 6:1–2 is represented in figure 1.

The brackets can also be portrayed by a series of arcs. If a passage is longer, it is easier to follow the argument with arcs rather than brackets. If the student studies the brackets closely, then it will be easy to see that the arc of the passage listed below is another way of portraying the passage (see fig. 2).

Third, the interpreter must explain the relationship between the different propositions. Writing out the explanation will ensure that the interpreter remembers how the text was understood. As one becomes more skilled in tracing the argument, this last step may become more apparent to the student, thereby making it unnecessary to write out the explanation.

Fig. 1 Bracketed Schema of 1 Tim. 6:1–2

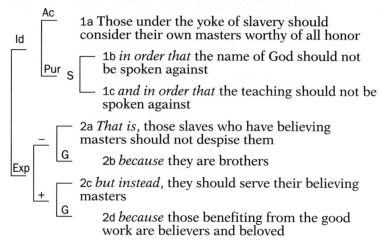

Now we proceed to the explanation of 1 Timothy 6:1–2. The way in which the text is indented indicates the main point in these two verses. The main point is given in the two commands in verses 1 and 2. In verse 1 Paul made the general point that slaves should honor their masters, and in verse 2 he explained more precisely what he had in mind in verse 1, namely, slaves should honor *believing* masters. Verse 2 clarifies the nature of the real problem, namely, Christian slaves who had believing masters were probably questioning whether they should submit to masters who were brothers in

Fig. 2 Arc Schema of 1 Tim. 6:1–2

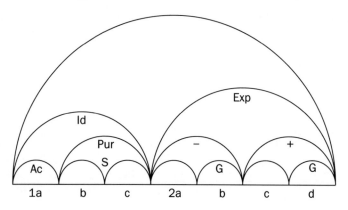

the faith. Thus, the relationship between verses 1–2 would be described as Idea-Explanation, and this is confirmed by the parallelism between the commands of the two verses, for to say that one "should not despise" a master (v. 2) is another way of saying that one "should consider a master worthy of all honor" (v. 1). Everything else in these two verses supports these two commands, and thus the rest of the propositions are indented to show that they function in a supporting way.

Now that we have seen the main proposition we can proceed with a more detailed analysis of verse one. The proposition in verse 1a clearly relates to 1b/1c as action-purpose. The action is given in 1a: slaves are to consider their masters as worthy of all honor. The reason or purpose for this action is given in 1b and 1c. Slaves are to honor their masters so that the name of God and the teaching of the gospel will not be spoken against and reviled. If believing slaves rebel against believing masters, the gospel message itself would be besmirched in the eyes of the unbelieving world. Thus, in 1b–c Paul supplied supporting propositions that explained why he thought it was so important to honor believing masters.

Both the name of God and the teaching are not to be blasphemed according to 1b and 1c. What is the relationship between the name of God and the teaching? The teaching does not seem to be climactic because it is unlikely that Paul thought the teaching was more important than God's name. Thus, the relation between 1b and 1c seems to be a series. Both the name of God and the teaching of the gospel should not be spoken against.

We have seen that the main proposition in verse 2, that slaves should not despise believing masters, is a further explanation of the main proposition in verse 1. The main proposition in verse 2 is explained by way of contrast, for 2a–b together function as the antithesis to 2c–d. Slaves are tempted to despise their Christian masters because these masters are brothers (2a–b), perhaps expecting better treatment or freedom from these masters. Paul used this same argument in 2c–d, however, for serving masters. They should serve masters all the more willingly because they are brothers! The relation between these two propositions is negative-positive: slaves should not despise Christian masters because they are brothers; instead, they should serve them all the more because they are brothers.

The remaining relationships to be analyzed in verse 2 are found in the relations between 2a and 2b, and 2c and 2d. The command in 2a is that those slaves who have believing masters should not despise their masters. Verse 2b provides the reason (ground) why Christian slaves would be tempted to despise believing masters: precisely because their masters were fellow-Christians they might be inclined to look down upon them. Perhaps these slaves expected their Christian owners to liberate them. In 2c Paul commanded slaves to serve their masters, and the ground or reason is given in 2d. Slaves should serve Christian masters for the very reason that these masters are brothers who will benefit from the slave's labor.

It may appear that tracing the logic in this way is a very laborious way to state what was obvious from the beginning. Even in short texts, however, this method is valuable because it constrains the reader to slow down and to note the function of every proposition in the text. The reader begins to observe more closely what is in the text, and then proceeds to ask questions about how the text coheres. In addition, the longer the text, the more such an analysis is necessary. It may be easy to consider the relationship between only two verses, but tracing the argument for extended paragraphs or even the entire letter can easily slip from our grasp unless we have some way of holding before our mind the logic of the text.

Example #2

We will present a more extended example from Romans 4:1–8 so that the reader can see how a longer passage is handled. The first step, once again, is to isolate the different propositions and to translate them.

1 *Therefore*, what shall we say that Abraham, our forefather according to the flesh, found?
2a *For if* Abraham was justified by works,
2b *then* he has a reason for boasting.
2c *But* he has no reason for boasting in God's sight.
    3a *For* the scripture says "Abraham believed God"
        3b *and as a consequence* his faith was counted to him as righteousness.

4 *Now let me explain further*: To the one who works wages are not counted as a gift but as a debt
5 *but* to the one who does not work but believes upon him who justifies the ungodly his faith is counted as righteousness

> 6 *just as* David also speaks of the blessing of the person to whom God counts righteousness apart from works
> 7a *He says*: Blessed is the person whose lawless deeds are forgiven
> 7b *and* his sins are covered over.
> 8 *And* Blessed is the person whose sin the Lord will not count.

Second, trace the argument of the passage to portray how the argument has been understood by putting in brackets or arcs (see fig. 3).

Third, explain the relationships between the different propositions. We need to say immediately that a number of exegetical issues cannot be discussed in this passage. For a detailed exegesis of this text, the reader should consult a commentary, such as Cranfield's on Romans (see appendix). The explanation that follows makes a number of assumptions regarding the meaning of the passage. Due to space restraints we will not attempt to defend all of these assumptions.[8]

The main proposition in Romans 4:1–8 is located in the answer to the question posed in verse 1. Here Paul inquired about the status of Abraham before God. The question arises because Paul has just contended that all people are justified by faith and not by the works of the law (Rom. 3:28). The one God does not justify Jews and Gentiles in a different way, for both are justified by faith (3:30). Paul's contention that all, both Jews and Gentiles, are justified by faith is flawed if Jews in the OT were justified by the works of the law. So in chapter 4 Paul anticipated a possible objection to the thesis of justification by faith presented at the close of chapter 3. Does the case of Abraham, the father of the Jewish nation, support the Pauline understanding of justification?

Now as we said above, the answer to the question posed in

---

8. D. P. Fuller (*Gospel and Law: Contrast or Continuum?* [Grand Rapids: Eerdmans, 1980], 105ff.) has significantly influenced my understanding of this text; however, I do not claim that he would necessarily agree with my analysis of this text.

Fig. 3   Propositional Schema of Rom. 4:1-8

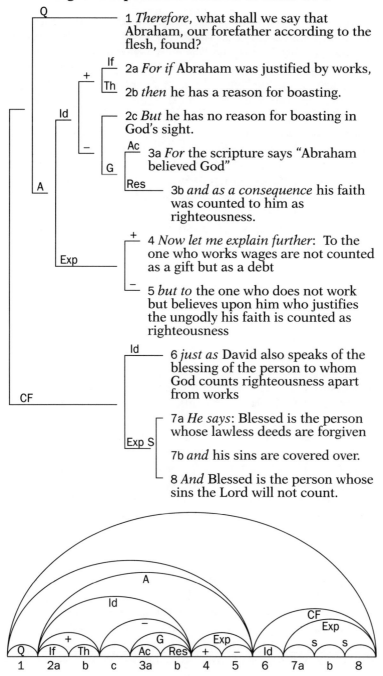

Q — 1 *Therefore*, what shall we say that Abraham, our forefather according to the flesh, found?

If — 2a *For if* Abraham was justified by works,

Th — 2b *then* he has a reason for boasting.

2c *But* he has no reason for boasting in God's sight.

Ac — 3a *For* the scripture says "Abraham believed God"

Res — 3b *and as a consequence* his faith was counted to him as righteousness.

+ — 4 *Now let me explain further*: To the one who works wages are not counted as a gift but as a debt

− — 5 *but to* the one who does not work but believes upon him who justifies the ungodly his faith is counted as righteousness

Id — 6 *just as* David also speaks of the blessing of the person to whom God counts righteousness apart from works

7a *He says*: Blessed is the person whose lawless deeds are forgiven

7b *and* his sins are covered over.

8 *And* Blessed is the person whose sins the Lord will not count.

119

verse 1 is the main proposition in this text. And the answer given in verses 2–5 is that Abraham has no grounds of boasting before God because he was counted righteous before God on the basis of his faith, not by his work for God. Therefore, Abraham supports Paul's claim in chapter 3 that both Jews and Gentiles are justified by faith. The example of David in verses 6–8 functions as a confirmatory argument for the same thesis. Paul introduced verse 6 with a comparative clause (καθάπερ, "just as"), demonstrating that David was justified *in the same way* as Abraham. David was counted righteous before God even though he was a sinner, even though works were lacking in his life. Thus, two of the most significant characters in Jewish history, Abraham and David, were not justified by working for God. They were counted righteous by believing God.

First, let us examine how Paul develops his argument regarding Abraham in verses 2–5. Paul acknowledged in verse 2 that *if* Abraham was righteous before God by virtue of his works, then he would have a reason to boast before God, and thus Paul's claim that boasting is excluded (Rom. 3:27) would be contradicted. The relationship between 2a and 2b is conditional: the main point here is that boasting is legitimate and warranted if Abraham has performed the necessary works.

Verses 2c–3b, however, function as the antithesis to the proposition in 2a–b. This antithesis is marked by the strong adversative "but" (ἀλλ', 4:2c). The main point of 2a–b is that Abraham can boast if he gained God's approval by working for him. But 2c–3b negates this assertion by saying that Abraham has no reason for boasting in God's sight. So 2a–b functions as a positive proposition: Abraham can boast if he has necessary works, while 2c–3b functions as a negative: Abraham has no reason to boast before God.

By isolating 2c–3b we can see that the main proposition here is that Abraham has no grounds for boasting before God. Paul needed to prove this assertion since it was the pivotal point in his argument. He cited Genesis 15:6 in verse 3 to ground his thesis. Note that verse 3 is indented above because it functions to support the proposition in 2c. Verse 3 is not the main point itself; instead, it functions as a support for the main point. How does verse 3 support Paul's main assertion in 2c? By citing the OT Paul defended his claim that justification is by faith. This OT text does not say that Abraham was right before God by his works. Rather, this text shows that Abraham's faith was the determinative factor in his justification. The relation between 3a and 3b is action-result. Abraham believed God, and the result or consequence of this belief was that God counted or reckoned this faith as righteousness. Abraham's righteousness was not the result of working for God; instead, it was the consequence of trusting God.

Now it seems to me that verses 4 and 5 function as a further explanation of verses 2–3. Before we see how verses 4 and 5 explain verses 2–3, the relationship between 4 and 5 should be investigated. It is easy to see that a negative-positive relation occurs between verses 4 and 5. Verse 4 says that one who works does not view his wages as a gift from the employer. Instead, the employee rightly thinks that his wages are deserved and his right since he has worked for them. On the other hand (verse 5), a person who does not work at all but merely believes is clearly in a different category than the person described in verse 4. He does not expect a reward from his own effort but looks to another for righteousness.

We are now in a position to see how verses 4–5 further explain verses 2–3. Verse 4 really functions as a further explication of verse 2. If Abraham worked for God as an employee, then what he did for God would surely deserve a reward since no employee views wages as a gift from the employer. And if Abraham did work for God in such a way that he deserved payment (v. 4), then he could boast (v. 2) that his justification was due to his working for God. But Paul affirms in verse 3 that Abraham was not justified by works; he was justified by trusting God. Verse 5 further explains what is involved in trusting God for righteousness. Saving faith recognizes that no one can work for God. Instead, saving faith trusts God to work for us. He justifies the ungodly. He makes ungodly sinners—like Abraham—what they were not previously, namely, righteous in God's sight. It is a great delusion for ungodly sinners to think that they can do anything to warrant God's approval. The faith that is counted for righteousness believes that strength is found only in God and humbly expects him to work for people.

We pointed out above that verses 6–8 function as a com-

parison to verses 1–5, showing that David was justified in the
same way that Abraham was. Righteousness was counted or
reckoned to David in the same way that it was counted to
Abraham. The main proposition in this section is found in
verse 6. David also recounts the blessing or happiness of the
person to whom righteousness is reckoned apart from working for God. The three propositions in verses 7–8 serve to
explain further the main idea found in verse 6. Thus, verse 6
is the idea and verses 7–8 are the explanation. In 7–8 Paul
cites Psalm 32:1–2, which picks up on the words "blessing"
and "count" used in verse 6. Indeed, the continued use of the
word "count" or "reckon" (λογίζομαι) also links this section
with 4:1–5.

The blessing of righteousness apart from works, therefore,
is recounted in Psalm 32:1–2. The three propositions in verses
7–8 seem to be a series in which each proposition says basi-
cally the same thing, but in different ways. The blessing of
justification is experienced when one's lawless deeds are forgiven. Another way of speaking of forgiveness is to say that
God covers over a person's sins (v. 7b). The last metaphor
used is one from accounting. God does not reckon or count a
person's sin against him. These citations from David's life con-
firm the central proposition that righteousness is not attained
by working for God. Righteousness is experienced when God
works for someone by forgiving lawless deeds, by covering
over past sins, and by not counting such infractions against
the person. David did not experience God's favor because he
was so noble that he did mighty things for God. Instead,
David experienced God's saving favor in spite of the fact that
he was a sinner. The fact that he needed forgiveness of sins
shows that he could not put God in his debt by doing good
works. Instead, God justified the ungodly David by forgetting
his sins. David was right before God because he believed in a
God who delights in working "for those who wait for him"
(Isa. 64:4).

Example #3

In our last example, Titus 2:1–10, for reasons of space we
will keep the explanation quite brief. First, we isolate the
propositions.

1 But you speak those things which are fitting for sound teaching.

2 *That is,* the older men should be sober, dignified, sensible, sound in faith, in love, and in endurance.

3a *And* in the same way, the older women should be reverent in their behavior

3b *That is,* they should not be slanderers, nor be enslaved to much wine, and they should be teachers of good.

> 4–5a *in order that* they should urge the younger women to love their husbands, to love their children, to be sensible, pure, workers at home, good, and submissive to their own husbands
>
> > 5b *in order that* the word of God should not be maligned.

6 *And* in the same way exhort the young men to be sensible

7a *in that* you show yourself as an example of good works in all things,

7b–8a *that is,* in your teaching show integrity, dignity, and healthy speech which is beyond reproach.

> 8b *in order that* our opponents should be ashamed
>
> > 8c *because* they have nothing evil to say about us.

9–10a *And* exhort slaves to be submissive to their own masters, to please them, to not speak back, to not steal, but instead to show all good faith,

> 10b *in order that* they might adorn the teaching of God our Savior in all things.

The series of commands within the individual verses above could be separated and presented in a series. Instead, I have chosen to include all of them as the object of what is commanded so that the larger structure of the text can be easily detected.

Second, we trace the argument between the different propositions (see fig. 4).

Third, we need to explain the structure of the text. Titus 2:1 is the topic sentence or the idea which is fleshed out in 2:2–10. In other words, the things that are fitting for sound teaching (v. 1) are explained in the admonitions to older men, older women, younger women, young men, and slaves in vv. 2–10. Note that the women are to live their lives in accordance with sound teaching "in the same way" (ὡσαύτως) as the older men. And the young men are exhorted to live "in the same way" as the older and younger women, and the older

Fig. 4 Propositional Schema of Titus 2:1–10

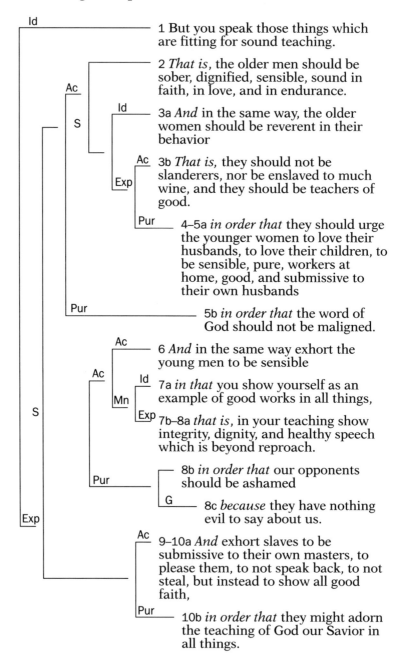

Id — 1 But you speak those things which are fitting for sound teaching.

Ac — **S** — 2 *That is*, the older men should be sober, dignified, sensible, sound in faith, in love, and in endurance.

Id — 3a *And* in the same way, the older women should be reverent in their behavior

Exp — **Ac** — 3b *That is*, they should not be slanderers, nor be enslaved to much wine, and they should be teachers of good.

Pur — 4–5a *in order that* they should urge the younger women to love their husbands, to love their children, to be sensible, pure, workers at home, good, and submissive to their own husbands

Pur — 5b *in order that* the word of God should not be maligned.

S — **Ac** — **Ac** — 6 *And* in the same way exhort the young men to be sensible

Mn — **Id** — 7a *in that* you show yourself as an example of good works in all things,

Exp — 7b–8a *that is*, in your teaching show integrity, dignity, and healthy speech which is beyond reproach.

Pur — 8b *in order that* our opponents should be ashamed

G — 8c *because* they have nothing evil to say about us.

Exp — **Ac** — 9–10a *And* exhort slaves to be submissive to their own masters, to please them, to not speak back, to not steal, but instead to show all good faith,

Pur — 10b *in order that* they might adorn the teaching of God our Savior in all things.

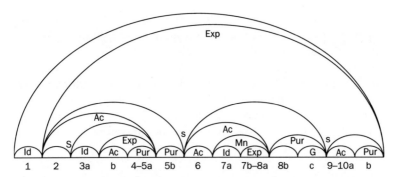

men. Even though the exhortations are introduced with a comparative word (ὡσαύτως), the text is probably better understood as a series of commands to these different groups.

In verse 3a Paul exhorted the older women to be reverent in their behavior, and in 3b he explained in more detail the nature of such reverent behavior. The ἵνα in 2:4 could be understood as a ἵνα of content further defining what it means to be a "teacher of what is good," or it could be a purpose ἵνα. I take it to be a purpose clause since in the pastoral Epistles both behavior and words are necessary for healthy teaching. Thus, the older women teach the younger women not only with words but by the way they live. The instructions given to the younger women are described in verses 4–5a.

The purpose clause in verse 5b at first glance seems to be attached only to the instructions given to the younger women. On the other hand, this purpose clause could possibly be understood as the purpose for all of verses 2–5. This latter view is strengthened by the use of a purpose clause to conclude the exhortations to young men and slaves in verses 8 and 10. If this latter view is the case, then it means that Paul concluded each major exhortation section in this passage with a purpose clause, explaining why he gave these exhortations. In each case he was concerned about the witness of believers in the world. By their good behavior they prevent the word of God from being maligned (v. 5b), they forestall any criticism of the gospel (v. 8c), and they make the teaching of the gospel attractive (v. 10b).

In Titus 2:6 Paul exhorted the young men to live sensibly. Interestingly, Paul said that Timothy should set an example for the younger men by his own life (2:7–8a). As the older

women should instruct the younger women with the beauty
of their lives, so Timothy should instruct the younger men by
his godly example of good works. In 2:7b–8a Paul specified
the good works he had in mind. We note again that Paul gave
the purpose for this exhortation in 8b, namely, that the opponents of the gospel should be ashamed. The ground or reason
for such shame is given in 8c, namely, the good works of
Timothy and the young men make it impossible for anything
evil to be said about them.

We have already pointed out that Paul exhorted slaves in
verses 9–10 and provided the purpose for such an exhortation. If we continued our analysis of the structure of this text,
it would be apparent that in 2:11–14 Paul provided the
ground for his instructions in 2:1–10 (note the γάρ ["for"] in
v. 11). The grace of God has appeared in Christ Jesus, and
thereby provides the motivation to live as new people.

Perhaps at this point the student is thinking, "Such
detailed work is too much, and there are other things to do in
life, too!" Admittedly, the task of trying to understand someone who wrote 2,000 years ago in a different language is not
an easy one. Certainly, careful study and disciplined reading
requires a great investment of time. Yet the rewards are great.
The pleasure of unlocking a text and knowing that one understands it is inexpressible. If time is a problem the wise student will spend it in the languages and in the texts. First hand
knowledge of Paul is the goal, not a derived knowledge that
cannot be evaluated. Commentaries can shed a great deal of
light on a text of Scripture, but I have found again and again
that careful study of the text will inevitably deal with the
same issues discussed in commentaries. And such intense
study provides the student with the necessary tools for evaluating the commentaries.

Of course, tracing logic is not the whole of exegesis. It is
dependent upon grammatical analysis as we have already
seen. But how we understand propositions is inevitably related to how we understand the words that make up the propositions. Thus, lexical study is imperative, and to this subject
we now turn.

7

Doing Lexical Studies

An objection could be raised here regarding the order of
the chapters. How can one understand propositions before
one understands the individual words contained in the propositions? Thus, it could be claimed that one should study the
meaning of terms in Paul before trying to comprehend the
relationship between different propositions. A few things can
be said in response to this anticipated objection. First, as recommended in chapter four, the interpreter should already
have looked up the meaning of words when translating the
passage being studied. Therefore, it would not be the case
that one would analyze propositions without any understanding of what individual words mean. Second, if one finds it
more helpful to study individual terms before diagramming
or tracing the argument, I have no great objection. It is true
that the understanding of a particular word or words may
cause one to understand the meaning of a proposition differ-
ently. Third, I have decided, however, to put the chapter on
lexical study in Paul here because the hermeneutical circle
functions in such a way that the context also plays a major
role in determining the meaning of an individual word.
Interpreters can also make serious mistakes in assigning a
particular meaning to a word without carefully understanding the entire context of a passage. The interpreter cannot
understand propositions without understanding the individual words that make up those propositions, and yet the mean-

ing of the propositions as a whole can also exert an impact on the meaning of individual words. The careful interpreter will always carefully consider the semantic range of a word and the particular context in which a word is used. Fourth, I placed this step here because studying words in Paul is a natural bridge to Pauline theology, and the issue of Pauline theology will be examined in the next chapter. During the history of the church, many of the words that Paul uses have rightly become crucial in the church's theology.

Lexical study is one of the most important elements of the exegetical process. Unfortunately, it is also an area that suffers from great abuse. Since many essays and books are available today that can help the student chart his way,[1] no one should commit egregious errors in this area any longer. I will not concentrate in this chapter on the general procedure or method of doing a lexical study. For this the student should refer to the introductory volume of this series, where Darrell Bock has laid out nicely the general procedure that should be followed.[2] Instead, this chapter will make a few observations regarding doing lexical studies in Paul.

Some Reflections on Lexical Study in Paul

Studying words in Paul can be distinguished from the same enterprise in the rest of the NT. In contrast to other NT authors, Paul wrote thirteen different pieces of literature. Thus, the interpreter has the opportunity to trace the meaning of a particular word through a number of letters. However, dangers lurk at every corner. For example, some students may pour too much meaning into Paul's words if they are not aware of the occasional nature of his correspondence. Indeed, the temptation is aggravated in the case of Paul precisely because his theology is so rich and thoughtful.

1. The works cited below move from the shortest and clearest expositions and progress to more technical studies: D. A. Carson, *Exegetical Fallacies* (Grand Rapids: Baker, 1984), 25–66; J. P. Louw, *Semantics of New Testament Greek* (Chico: Scholars, 1982); A. Thiselton, "Semantics and New Testament Interpretation," in *New Testament Interpretation* ed. I. H. Marshall (Grand Rapids: Eerdmans, 1977), 75–104; J. Barr, *The Semantics of Biblical Language* (Oxford: Oxford University Press, 1961); M. Silva, *Biblical Words and Their Meaning: An Introduction to Lexical Semantics* (Grand Rapids: Zondervan, 1983).

2. D. L. Bock, "New Testament Word Analysis," in *Introducing New Testament Interpretation*, ed. Scot McKnight (Grand Rapids: Baker, 1989), 97–113.

The student should recall that Paul did not write systematic treatises. His letters were occasional, responding to specific situations in the churches (we shall have more to say about this in our next chapter on constructing a Pauline theology). The point here is that the student should beware of assuming that Paul used his terms technically. He did not write precise philosophical treatises in which he attempted to define precisely the meaning of each term. For example, one might conclude that the word "works" in the plural (ἔργα) is always negative in Paul because: (1) he often insists that one cannot be justified "by works of the law" (ἐξ ἔργων νόμου, Rom. 3:20; Gal. 2:16 [3 times]; 3:2, 5, 10; cf. Rom. 3:28); (2) he speaks negatively of "works" (ἔργα) in general without mentioning the law (Rom. 4:2, 6; 9:12, 32; 11:6); and (3) when he speaks of a good work he often uses the singular ἔργον (Rom. 2:7, 15; 13:3; 14:20; 15:18; 1 Cor. 3:13–15; 9:1; 15:58; 16:1; etc.). Nevertheless, Paul can use the plural "works" (ἔργα) in a positive sense in some contexts (e.g., Rom. 2:6; Eph. 2:10; 1 Tim. 2:10; 5:10, 25; 6:18; Titus 2:7; 3:8, 14). Indeed, these texts show that Paul thought that good works were ultimately crucial for salvation. It is simplistic to assign a negative meaning to "works" in Paul from a selective citation of the evidence. What Paul meant in any given instance by ἔργα must be determined from the context, not from any preconceived notion that Paul thought of "works" in only one way. The careful interpreter seeks to decipher the difference between Paul's negative and positive understanding of ἔργα.

This same error of defining words too technically in Pauline literature can be illustrated in another way. In Colossians 1:26–27, Paul defined "mystery" (μυστήριον) as "Christ in you, the hope of glory." In Ephesians 3:4–6, however, Paul understood the "mystery" that was revealed as the the unity and solidarity of Jews and Gentiles in Christ. The Gentiles are "heirs together with Israel, members together of one body, and sharers together in the promise in Christ Jesus" (Eph. 3:6). Now one would have to ignore the context of Ephesians if one wanted to insist that the meaning of "mystery" in Ephesians is the same as that in Colossians. There is no a priori reason why Paul needed to use the same word in the same way when writing two different letters, or even within the same letter. The new perspective given to the word "mystery" in Ephesians may be due to Paul's purpose in writing that particular letter to early Christian communities.

Paul's flexibility with words and metaphors should be illustrated again since so many students, including some NT scholars, have a view of Paul that is too wooden. In 1 Corinthians 3:11 Paul said, "no one can lay any foundation other than the one already laid, which is Jesus Christ." But in Ephesians 2:20 Paul said that the church is "built on the foundation of the apostles and prophets, with Christ Jesus himself as the chief cornerstone." What Paul meant by "the foundation of the apostles and prophets" could be interpreted in various ways, but some think that this assertion contradicts the statement in 1 Corinthians 3:11 which refers to Jesus Christ as the only foundation. Because of this divergence (and other reasons as well) some deny the Pauline authorship of Ephesians. Incidentally, some who opt for Pauline authorship of Colossians have difficulty with Ephesians being Pauline, and one of the reasons being given is that the word "mystery" is used in a different sense.

Such an approach to words and metaphors in Paul is too rigid and should be discarded. Paul felt at liberty to use the metaphor of the foundation of the church in various ways. He had an artistic and creative mind and was not writing treatises in which every word and metaphor was used in a rigorously consistent fashion (I wonder if any writer of such treatises is so consistent!). Indeed, there is no material difference between 1 Corinthians 3:11 and Ephesians 2:20. In the latter, Jesus is the cornerstone of the building, which is another way of saying that he is the essential component of the building, and that is what the metaphor of the foundation in 1 Corinthians 3:11 communicates as well.

One of the most common errors committed when interpreting Paul, then, is to assume that he invariably coined technical terms. However, since Paul was a flexible and adaptable writer, the meaning of each word must be investigated carefully in its context. Also, the reader should keep in mind that Paul addressed his letters to specific communities. On the other hand, one could mistakenly assume that Paul embraced a wide range of different meanings for the same word, but some words in Paul may be used with the same meaning from letter to letter. If the basic semantic range of a word suggests a particular meaning, then that semantic range should be abandoned only if there are traits in a particular context that demand the adoption of a new meaning.

When attempting to determine the meaning of a given word in Paul, one should first use a concordance to locate every occurrence of the word. Besides the NT text itself, I think that a concordance is the single most important tool for a student. Because it is so important, I recommend that students buy the concordance edited by Bachmann and Slaby, even though it is quite expensive.[3] When using the concordance, first check for other occurrences of the word in the same letter and then in other Pauline letters. The order here is important. Since the same letter is the more immediate context, the student should consult it first. Then the student should check the rest of Paul's letters to determine the precise Pauline usage.

At this point it may be helpful to provide an example of a concordance study in which Paul used a term in a consistent way. In reading 1 Corinthians 9:27 I wondered what Paul meant by the word ἀδόκιμος. There he spoke of mistreating his body and bringing it into subjection so that he should not be ἀδόκιμος after preaching to others. Some scholars have suggested that when Paul used this word he was speaking of losing his reward but not the danger of apostasy. I had also understood the passage in the same way.[4] Then I wondered if

3. Computer-Concordance zum Novum Testamentum Graece von Nestle–Aland, 26. Auflage, und zum Greek New Testament, 3d ed. (Berlin: Walter de Gruyter, 1980). If the student simply cannot afford to purchase this volume, then he or she should purchase Moulton and Geden, although it is based on an inferior Greek text: W. F. Moulton and A. S. Geden, A Concordance to the Greek Testament According to the Texts of Westcott and Hort, Tischendorf and the English Revisers, 5th rev. ed. with supplement (Edinburgh: T. & T. Clark, 1978). Kurt Aland has also edited a two-volume concordance, the first of which uses a superscript system to access certain constructions and idioms. The second volume contains valuable statistical data. Unfortunately, these volumes are so expensive that only a student close to a theological library that has these can realistically expect to use them: K. Aland, ed., Vollständige Konkordanz zum Griechischen Neuen Testament: Zugrundellegung aller kritischen Textausgaber und des Textus Receptus, 2 vols. (Berlin: Walter de Gruyter, 1975–1983). For the student who struggles greatly with Greek, the subsequent work may be a bridge tool until the student acquires more skill in Greek: G. V. Wigram and J. P. Green, Sr., The New Englishman's Greek Concordance and Lexicon (Peabody, Mass.: Hendrickson, 1986). This is a new and revised edition of the old Wigram's, the 9th edition of which was published in 1903. The advantage of this tool is that every Greek word in the NT is listed in alphabetical order along with a brief English rendering of every verse in which that Greek word appears. This concordance is based on the Textus Receptus.

4. For this interpretation, see L. Morris, The First Epistle of Paul to the Corinthians (Grand Rapids: Eerdmans, 1958), 140.

this was correct since the example of Israel in the wilderness (1 Cor. 10:1–13) and the strong words about sharing the table of demons (10:19–22) suggested that Paul was speaking about something more serious than simply losing rewards.[5] The immediate context (step 1 above) suggests that ἀδόκιμος refers to being disqualified before God at the day of judgment, that is, Paul buffeted himself so that he would not suffer eternal punishment.

A concordance study shows that Paul did not use this word anywhere else in 1 Corinthians; however, it does appear six other times in Pauline literature. In each case Paul used it clearly in reference to *unbelievers* (Rom. 1:28; 2 Cor. 13:5, 6, 7; 2 Tim. 3:8; Titus 1:16). Particularly interesting is 2 Corinthians 13:5, where Paul said, "Recognize that Jesus Christ is in you unless you are unapproved [ἀδόκιμος]." According to Paul no one has the Spirit of Christ (Rom. 8:9) unless he or she is a believer. So Paul's statement in 2 Corinthians 13:5 could be construed as follows: "If Jesus Christ is *not* in you, then you are unapproved [i.e., unsaved]." Concordance study confirmed the suggestion from context that in 1 Corinthians 9:27 Paul was speaking of the threat of apostasy, of falling from the faith and toward destruction.

In summary, sometimes the meaning of a word can change the meaning of the entire passage. Thus, careful attention to the context and to Pauline usage elsewhere is crucial to accurate interpretation.[6]

Selecting Words to Study

One of the crucial issues in studying terms in Paul is the selection of words for further study. Certainly, no one has enough time to study each word, so an intelligent selection of words for further study is crucial. No fail-safe rules can be given for selecting words since each passage is different, but the following suggestions may help the interpreter to begin the process.

5. See G. D. Fee, *The First Epistle to the Corinthians* (Grand Rapids: Eerdmans, 1987), 433–75, for detailed support for such an exegesis of this passage.

6. I am not denying the importance of studying the usage of the same words elsewhere outside of the Pauline corpus. See D. Bock's essay in the introductory volume of this series (see note 2 above) for the proper procedure.

First, study words that are theologically significant. Sometimes students assume that they already know what χάρις, δικαιο–σύνη, ἐλπίς, and other theologically weighty words mean in Paul, and thus they never study foundational words. They assume that the way these words are defined in their systematic theology is correct. This is no criticism of systematic theology, for the theologian may be precisely right in assigning a definition for the word in question. However, the student needs to know from a firsthand analysis of the text what Paul means by grace, righteousness, and hope.

For example, opinions differ over what Paul meant when he used the word δικαιοσύνη?[7] Did he use it forensically to speak of our righteous status before God? Or did he use δικαιοσύνη with a transformative sense to indicate that God's righteousness is both a gift and a power that transforms us? My intention here, of course, is not to enter into the debate. Here the point is that the student must study δικαιοσύνη on his or her own. No meaningful evaluation of the various interpretations of righteousness can be rendered unless one has carefully studied the word in the contexts in which Paul used it.[8]

Second, one should study words that occur often in a passage and contribute to a major theme. For example, in 1 Corinthians 1:17–2:16 Paul's conception of σοφία is obviously of major importance since he used the word fifteen times in this text. In 1 Corinthians 1:18ff. the meaning of "calling" (κλητοῖς, v. 24; κλῆσιν, v. 26) can be grasped more keenly if

7. The literature on this topic is voluminous. For a start, see E. R. Achtemeier, "Righteousness in the OT," in *The Interpreter's Dictionary of the Bible*, ed. G. A. Buttrick (Nashville: Abingdon, 1962), 4:80–85; P. J. Achtemeier, "Righteousness in the NT," *The Interpreter's Dictionary of the Bible*, 4:91–99; G. Klein, "Righteousness in the NT," *The Interpreter's Dictionary of the Bible, Supplementary Volume*, ed. K. Crim et al. (Nashville: Abingdon, 1976), 750–52; E. Käsemann, "God's Righteousness in Paul," *Journal of Theology and Church* 1 (1965): 100–10; R. Bultmann, "ΔΙΚΑΙΟΣΥΝΗ ΘΕΟΥ," *Journal of Biblical Literature* 83 (1964): 12–16; J. A. Ziesler, *The Meaning of Righteousness in Paul: A Linguistic and Theological Enquiry* (Cambridge: At the University Press, 1972); D. Hill, *Greek Words and Hebrew Meanings* (Cambridge: At the University Press, 1967), 82–162; J. Reumann, *Righteousness in the New Testament* (Philadelphia: Fortress, 1982); M. T. Brauch, "Appendix: Perspectives on 'God's Righteousness' in Recent German Discussion," in *Paul and Palestinian Judaism: A Comparison of Patterns of Religion* (Philadelphia: Fortress, 1977), 523–42; P. Stuhlmacher, "The Apostle Paul's View of Righteousness," in *Reconciliation, Law, & Righteousness: Essays in Biblical Theology* (Philadelphia: Fortress, 1986), 68–93.

8. The use of the word in the OT and during the intertestamental period also plays a key role in the debate.

one notices that it is contrasted with κηρύσσομεν in 1:23, and is equated with ἐξελέξατο in 1:27–28. Since "calling" is implicitly distinguished from "preaching," "calling" cannot be identified as an invitation to believe the gospel. Indeed, Paul described "calling" in terms of God's choice of the Corinthians (1:27–28). Thus, Paul used the word "calling" here to refer to God's sovereign and effective choice by which he brings believers into fellowship with himself (see 1 Cor. 1:9).[9] In 2 Corinthians 1:3–7 the noun and verb form of παρακαλέω occur ten times. A word cries out for examination when it is so prominent. Thus, careful observation of a text will help the interpreter note words that recur often and that have potential significance for the interpretation of a given passage.

Third, one should study words with debated meanings that are crucial for the understanding of a given passage. For example, did Paul assert that the husband is the *authority over* his wife or that he is the *source of* his wife? The argument hangs on the meaning of the Greek word κεφαλή in Paul, a topic that is vigorously debated today (1 Cor. 11:3–16; Eph. 5:22–24; etc.).[10] Also, did Paul use the word σκεῦος in 1 Thessalonians 4:4 in reference to one's body or to one's wife? If the former, then Paul was exhorting the Thessalonians to control their bodies in a sexually honorable way. If the latter, then Paul was exhorting the Thessalonians to acquire a wife in a sexually honorable way.

---

9. A concordance study of καλέω, κλητός, and κλῆσις shows that this is a common meaning for these words in Paul. The careful reader will notice the tension here between my understanding of "calling" and the comments made on apostasy earlier. I think a resolution of this tension is possible, but for reasons of space it will not be attempted here.

10. For representative positions in the debate, see B. and A. Mickelsen, "What Does Kephalē Mean in the New Testament?" in *Women, Authority & the Bible* (Downers Grove, Ill.: InterVarsity, 1986), 97–110; W. Grudem, "Does κεφαλή Mean 'Source' or 'Authority Over' in Greek Literature? A Survey of 2,336 Examples," *Trinity Journal* 6 (1985): 38–59; R. S. Cervin, "Does Κεφαλή Mean 'Source' or 'Authority Over' in Greek Literature? A Rebuttal," *Trinity Journal* 10 (1989): 85–112.

8

Probing
the Theological Context

From the outset of the book we acknowledged that the cap-
stone of exegesis is theological synthesis. Every person lives
from his or her worldview, which is another way of saying
that every one lives from his or her theology. It follows, then,
that the importance of the theological context in the Pauline
letters can hardly be exaggerated.

The Pauline letters present a unique challenge theologically
because we possess, assuming all the letters are authentic,
thirteen letters by him. No other NT writer presents quite the
same challenge. Of course, Luke and John also wrote substantial parts of the NT, but their writings come in bigger blocks,
not in thirteen different pieces of literature.[1]

We have already noted that Paul wrote his letters to
address specific situations in the churches. This raises the
question of whether it is even possible to discover a Pauline
theology. Are Paul's letters exclusively pastoral responses to
specific problems? And if so, does not the very attempt to
construct a Pauline theology impose an alien form upon
Paul's thought? Did Paul, in writing his various letters, coun-
teract errors manifesting themselves in his churches without
considering whether what he wrote in one letter harmonized
with what he wrote in others? Was Paul simply a "fireman"

1. In addition, the authorship of various Johannine writings is disputed. And because
2–3 John are so brief they are not that fruitful for constructing a Johannine theology.

putting out "fires" in the churches without having a coherent philosophy of "fire prevention"?

J. Christian Beker's distinction between the *coherent center* of Paul's thought and his *contingent* instructions for the various churches is helpful here.[2] Paul did not spin out systematic theological treatises in his letters. He usually responded to specific circumstances that were occurring in the churches. Nevertheless, Paul's response to the churches is not adequately described as ad hoc only. Paul did give specific advice to churches struggling with various problems, but his advice issued from a coherent theological worldview.[3] Paul applied his theological worldview to the situations which arose. His letters would not be so profound if he were merely a pragmatist reacting to the situations occurring in the churches. The profundity of his thought reveals itself in the pastoral application of his theology to concrete situations. The task of the interpreter is to work back from the specific letters to the formation of Paul's theological worldview. Naturally we do not have enough information in these letters to determine Paul's view on every theological issue, but there is enough information to provide the reader with a very full-blooded picture of Paul's theology.

Contradictions in Pauline Theology?

Some scholars, on the other hand, maintain that Paul's theology is not coherent. The most prominent contemporary example of this perspective occurs in the stimulating work of H. Räisänen.[4] Räisänen thinks that Paul's theology on the law is incoherent and contradictory. Presumably he would not be surprised to find contradictions in other areas of Paul's theology as well.[5] Räisänen does not think Paul was intellectually vacuous. Paul was saddled with certain cultural and psycho-

---

2. J. C. Beker, *Paul the Apostle: The Triumph of God in Life and Thought* (Philadelphia: Fortress, 1980), 11–17; see his recent article, "Paul's Theology: Consistent or Inconsistent," *New Testament Studies* 34 (1988): 364–77.

3. It should be noted that Beker, although he sees coherence in Paul's gospel, does not think Paul is as consistent as I take him to be.

4. *Paul and the Law* (Philadelphia: Fortress, 1986).

5. For a similar view in Paul's theology of predestination, see H. Räisänen, *The Idea of Divine Hardening: A Comparative Study of the Notion of Divine Hardening, Leading Astray and Inciting to Evil in the Bible and the Qur'an* (Helsinki: Finnish Exegetical Society, 1976).

logical commitments to Judaism and the OT that compelled
him to reconcile his new experience of Jesus with the OT
Scriptures. Such an attempted reconciliation, Räisänen thinks,
is impossible. Therefore, Paul rationalized the OT Scriptures
and ended up affirming things that simply contradict one
another. Räisänen's arguments cannot be dismissed. They
must be seriously considered and evaluated. He raises all the
right questions, and crisply poses some of the major problems
in reconciling Paul's thought.

We cannot evaluate in any detail here Räisänen's arguments.[6] I think it is fair to say that he does not give Paul a
sympathetic reading. It seems that he tries to see diversity in
Paul's thought wherever possible. A sympathetic reading can
often yield satisfying solutions to the problems raised by
Paul's apparently conflicting statements. The crucial issue
here is one of perspective. One can make sense of Paul by
positing contradictions in his thought or by defending his
theology as harmonious. I think the interpreter should proceed from the assumption that Paul's thought is coherent and
consistent unless there is compelling evidence to the contrary.
Of course, Räisänen believes that he has provided such evidence to the contrary.

Perhaps one example, which I have mentioned elsewhere,[7]
will illustrate the point at hand. Räisänen says that Paul's
theology of law is contradictory because in one place Paul
said that the law is abolished, and yet in other places Paul
said that the law should be fulfilled by Christians (Rom.
7:1–6; Gal. 3:15–4:7; 2 Cor. 3:7ff.; cf. Rom. 13:8–10; Gal.
5:14).[8] Now Paul did make such astonishingly diverse statements which cause any interpreter to wonder if Paul's thinking does cohere. But to posit a contradiction at this point
should be rejected as an overly simplistic solution to the problem. A very interesting text in this regard is 1 Corinthians 7:19
where Paul said, "Circumcision is nothing and uncircumci-
sion is nothing. Keeping God's commands is what counts."
Now this text is surprising because circumcision is one of the
commandments of God! The OT clearly commanded it (Gen.

6. For a recent response to Räisänen, see C. E. B. Cranfield, "Giving a Dog a Bad
Name: A Note on H. Räisänen's *Paul and the Law*," *Journal for the Study of the New
Testament* 38 (1990): 77–85.

7. "The Abolition and Fulfillment of the Law in Paul," *Journal for the Study of the
New Testament* 35 (1989): 47–48.

8. Räisänen, *Paul and the Law*, 42–73.

17:9–14), and yet Paul distinguished it from the divine commandments. Nevertheless, Paul also stressed the importance of obeying the commandments. In the same verse Paul affirmed the abiding validity of the law and dismissed some of the law. This indicates that Paul's view on the abolition and fulfillment of the law is complex. One should not assume too quickly that he contradicted himself, for it is very unlikely that a person like Paul, who was raised on the Scriptures, would not see that 1 Corinthians 7:19 contained an apparent contradiction. My point is that the alleged contradictions in Paul can be explained, and that there are indications that Paul himself was aware of the complexity of his thought.

Since Paul was clearly an intelligent person, we should grant him the benefit of the doubt on the issue of consistency. Many intelligent interpreters have perceived a profound consistency and coherence in Paul. This provides a safe starting point for the interpreter.

Development in Pauline Theology

Another possibility is that Paul's theology developed as he grew in maturity and experience. Paul's letters, in this view, would not necessarily have any internal contradictions, but it would be wrong to assume that his letters would contain a consistent theology because Paul changed his mind on some matters as time progressed.[9] The contradictions would not be

9. Among those who see developments in Paul's theology are C. H. Dodd, "The Mind of Paul: Change and Development," *Bulletin of the John Rylands Library* 18 (1934): 69–110; C. H. Buck and G. Taylor, *Saint Paul: A Study of the Development of His Thought* (New York: Scribner, 1969); J. W. Drane, *Paul, Libertine or Legalist? A Study of the Theology of the Major Pauline Epistles* (London: SPCK, 1975); and H. Hübner, *Law in Paul's Thought* (Edinburgh: T. & T. Clark, 1984). R. N. Longenecker ("On the Concept of Development in Pauline Thought," in *Perspectives on Evangelical Theology*, ed. K. S. Kantzer and S. N. Gundry [Grand Rapids: Baker, 1979], 195–207) understood development in Paul in terms of growth from a seed into a flower. The flower of Paul's thought would not be identical with the seed in every respect and there would be developments in the flower which were not apparent in the seed, but the flower would in no way contradict what was in the seed. The flower would manifest more fully what was inherent in the seed from the beginning. This understanding of development is quite different from that which we are contesting. It is altogether likely that Paul's thought did develop in the way described by Longenecker. Nevertheless, I am less sanguine than Longenecker about the possibility of tracing such development in Paul's letters. Paul's theology probably developed most significantly before he began writing any letters, and thus tracing the development of Pauline theology in the extant letters is not easily demonstrable, and the reasons for this difficulty are the same as those given against other theories of development.

within the same letter but *between* the different letters. The word "contradiction" is probably too strong of a word to describe this position since Paul simply changed his mind on something he previously believed. Two examples of this type of development in Paul's theology are given below.

First, some scholars have argued that Paul changed his eschatology.[10] Originally, Paul thought that he would live until the day of the parousia (1 Thess. 4:13–18). He expected to be on earth when Jesus came again, and thus he would experience the resurrection of his body at the parousia. After Paul experienced a great crisis in his life (probably reflected in 2 Cor. 1:8–11), he began to reckon with the possibility that he would not live until the parousia. He also changed his view of the resurrection, asserting now that believers would receive their resurrection body at death instead of at the parousia (2 Cor. 5:1–10).

Second, another example of development in Paul comes from Paul's theology of the law. Hans Hübner argued that in Galatians Paul abolished the law altogether.[11] Nothing positive is asserted with respect to the Torah. In fact, Paul even attributed the origin of the law to demons (Gal. 3:19–20). In Romans, however, Paul moderated his view of the law. No longer did he think that the law was wholly abolished. Instead, the law was abolished insofar as it was abused and misused. The law itself, according to Romans, was good. Hübner suggested that Paul came to this more moderate position on the law after James the brother of Jesus communicated to Paul how extreme the latter's views were and the negative impact Paul's argument in Galatians would have on the Jewish brethren.

The developmental view of Paul's theology is not convincing for a several reasons.[12]

First, it does not account satisfactorily for the fact that Paul had been a missionary at least fifteen years before writ-

10. The most notable adherent of this view is C. H. Dodd, "Change and Development," 69–110.

11. See note 9 above for bibliographic information.

12. For a review of Buck and Taylor, see V. P. Furnish, "Review of C. H. Buck and G. Taylor, *Saint Paul: A Study of the Development of His Thought*," *Journal of the American Academy of Religion* 38 (1970): 289–303. For problems with the developmental view, see J. Lowe, "An Examination of Attempts to Detect Developments in St. Paul's Theology," *Journal of Theological Studies* 42 (1941): 129–42; Räisänen, *Paul and the Law*, 7–10.

ing any of his letters. By the time he started writing his letters, he had probably hammered out the major issues in his
theology.

Second, due consideration must be given to Paul's
Pharisaic background. He was a person who had studied the
Scriptures assiduously before his conversion. One of the
objections he probably raised against Jesus being Messiah
was that a crucified man was cursed by God (Deut. 21:23; see
Gal. 3:13), and thus could never be the Messiah. Upon his
conversion the Pharisaic Paul surely would have started to
rethink his view of the law immediately. He would need to
explain from the Torah how a crucified man could be the
Messiah.

Third, most developmental schemas founder because Paul's
letters cannot be dated with precision. For example, it is
unclear whether Galatians was written in the late 40s or the
middle 50s. It is impossible to delineate the stages of Paul's
thought unless there is more certainty regarding the dating of
each letter. Furthermore, even if one could date the letters
with more precision, they were written in such close proximi-
ty to each other that it is difficult to see how a developmental
schema can be sustained.

Fourth, most developmental views engage in speculative
historical reconstructions like Hübner's theory that Paul
changed his mind on the law after hearing from James. There
is not a shred of evidence for this reconstruction, and such
alleged events place the whole building of development on a
shaky foundation.

Fifth, it is much more likely that the differences between
the writings can be explained by the occasional nature of the
letters. As we have pointed out before, Paul's view of the law
in Galatians seemed more negative because he was opposing
legalists. Paul would not have emphasized the value of the
law when confronting people who overestimated its importance. Those who see development in Paul's letters rightly discern the different emphases in Paul's letters. The diversity of
the letters should be assigned, however, to the occasion to
which Paul responds and not to the development of his theology.

Advantages and Dangers
of Probing the Theological Context

What we have been arguing for is the idea that Paul's theology should be taken as a whole. He was a coherent and consistent thinker. The danger of not doing any theological synthesis is a simplistic biblicism. All attempts to systematize
Paul are rejected, and the interpreter claims to be doing biblical rather than systematic theology. But biblical theology, if it
is to have any coherence, must work with the law of noncontradiction, and it must try to construct some kind of coherent
system out of Paul's theology. Otherwise, the interpreter is
simply left with a hodgepodge of passages. The failure to
think through Paul's theology systematically can prevent one
from thinking profoundly enough about his thought.

I think it is also true that we may understand individual
passages in Paul better as we comprehend the whole of Paul's
theology with more precision. This is often denied today.
Some interpreters have suggested that it is methodologically
flawed to utilize Romans to understand what Paul is saying in
Galatians.[13] Each letter should be interpreted as if we did not
possess the others. It is sometimes said that only this method
will ensure objectivity.

It is true, of course, that we should not impose Romans on
Galatians (more on this below). We should be open to the distinctive message of each letter. Nevertheless, it is artificial to
separate the letters from one another and to isolate each letter from the living Paul. I have found that the more I read of
C. S. Lewis, the more I understand him. By reading his essays
and expository works I gain a better grasp of his novels and
children's stories. The same themes appear in a different
guise, and because I have read Lewis elsewhere I understand
more clearly what he means. The same is true of Paul and
most human authors. The more one reads of Paul, the fuller
picture one gets of his thinking. Passages in Romans can help
one understand Paul's statements in Galatians. The attempt to
separate each letter from one another produces a bloodless
Paul. It unintentionally dehumanizes Paul by separating the
author from each of his literary works. Our ability to understand other human beings increases with more exposure. For

13. See H. D. Betz, *A Commentary on Paul's Letter to the Churches in Galatia*
(Philadelphia: Fortress, 1979), xv–xvi; also see p. 146.

example, the more classes we take from a teacher, the better
we understand that teacher. Thus, the way we interpret most
authors and teachers should also be the way we interpret
Paul.

Doing theological synthesis in Paul also has dangers. We
may fail to hear what a particular text is saying because that
text has already been swallowed up into our system. The
problem here is not with systematizing, but with a system
that is not comprehensive enough, with a system that does
not take into account all the facts. Thus, we may fail to let
particular texts change our view of Pauline theology. We all
come to the text with certain assumptions and desires about
the meaning of the biblical text. Thus, it is extraordinarily
easy to read into the text our own meaning. Any theological
synthesis that fails to account for the particulars of specific
texts is unsatisfactory.

As we form a coherent view of Paul's theology we should
not be afraid to change our mind. We are all learning and
growing, and our knowledge is partial. No one sees the whole
picture adequately, and yet we keep straining to see it better.
That is part of the process and excitement of learning. New
issues and situations rightly call us to reexamine the text to
see if we have misunderstood what Paul was saying. Paul was
a profound and complex theologian, and also one of the most
important both historically and for the life of the church
today. We should expect that studying a great thinker like
Paul will take time and effort. Along the way we will probably
even discover that we have not always interpreted him correctly. We hope that as time progresses our knowledge of
Pauline theology will deepen. We also hope that as we under-
gird our theological reflection with careful exegesis we will
gain confidence in our interpretation of Pauline theology.

Investigating Pauline Theology

How should we probe the theological context in Paul? How
should we approach the task of theological synthesis? We all
start with certain preconceptions when we read Paul. From
previous readings of Paul we have become convinced that he
taught and believed various doctrines. There is nothing wrong
with such assumptions about Pauline theology. It would be
very difficult to interpret Paul if we had to rethink every issue

afresh in Pauline theology each time we read him! Theological synthesis occurs by asking larger questions about Pauline teaching in light of particular texts. For example, one might assert that Paul believed that justification was by faith and not by works. Paul plainly said that God justifies the ungodly (Rom. 4:5). Yet he also said that those who practice evil will not enter into the kingdom (Gal. 5:19–21; 1 Cor. 6:9–11). Apparently works do play some role in justification. How then do the two emphases on faith and works complement each other? Particular texts that seem to contradict one's previous notions about Pauline theology motivate us to reexamine what Paul really thought.

Now if one were reading Paul with no idea at all about what he taught elsewhere, then such questions would not even arise. If one had no conviction about the Pauline theology of justification, then the assertion that good works are necessary for justification may simply strike one as an obvious truth. The fact is, however, that a person without any previous experience in interpreting Paul is simply not ready to ask the most profound questions about Pauline theology. Someone who has read and understood Paul's theology about justification by faith and who reads with discernment will surely puzzle over the assertion that obedience is necessary for justification (see Rom. 2:6–11, 25–29; 1 Cor. 9:24–10:22; 2 Cor. 5:10). Someone who has not been perplexed at all by such diverse statements is really at a very elementary level in reading Paul. Perplexity surfaces when apparently irreconcilable statements are made. Good theology begins then with a questioning mind.

I am emphasizing this point because I have heard some people exalt a theologically blank mind as a virtue. It is not a virtue, but a disadvantage, albeit a disadvantage that can be removed through study of the text. For the person who holds certain preconceptions about Pauline theology the only disadvantage is closing his mind and ceasing to ask questions. Such a person will cease to learn, and the subsequent atrophying of the mind of this person will be obvious to those around him. Putting together Paul's theology comes from being disturbed and confused about how it all fits together. That leads a person on the exciting quest of trying to find solutions. Those who have curious minds and ask questions will inevitably probe more deeply into Paul's theology.

Of course, we ask questions to get answers and to discover the most satisfactory answers to the hard questions. No one can claim to understand Paul's theology perfectly, but surely we can gain a substantial and significant comprehension of his thinking. I am not suggesting that we must reopen an issue in Pauline theology whenever someone questions it. However, when the question raises issues that have not been solved by previous investigations, then we are obligated to reexamine the issue. Since each one of us inclines toward prejudice in our views, we should listen with extraordinary care to any objections to the views we espouse. Such objections may be the path to more precise and satisfying solutions.

Doing Pauline theology, then, does not begin with a starting point outside of Paul. It is a process of wrestling with diverse statements made by Paul and trying to discover the unity that undergirds the diversity of his expression. Two examples of tensions that surface in Paul's thinking have already been mentioned in this chapter: the issue of the abrogation and fulfillment of the law, and the relationship between works and justification. But many other questions also surface when one reads Paul. First Corinthians 10:1–13 seems to threaten believers with final judgment if they apostasize. But didn't Paul say elsewhere that God will finish the good work he started (Phil. 1:6) and that nothing can separate us from the love of Christ (Rom. 8:35–39)? How could he threaten believers with destruction if they fall away, and yet at the same time assure them that nothing will prevent them from inheriting salvation?

Paul claimed that the wall of hostility has been broken down between Jews and Gentiles (Eph. 2:11–22) and that there is no distinction between Jew and Greek (Gal. 3:28). But if this is so how could he posit a future eschatological salvation for ethnic Israel in Romans 11? Doesn't this raise again the old barriers between Jews and Gentiles? Doesn't this give an advantage to Israel that Paul has argued elsewhere she doesn't possess?

What shall we say about Paul's view of women? In one place he affirmed that in Christ there is no distinction

between men and women (Gal. 3:28). But elsewhere he forbade women to teach and he seemed to place them under the
authority of men (1 Cor. 11:3–16; 14:33b–36; Eph. 5:22–33;
Col. 3:18; 1 Tim. 2:11–15). Is there any coherence to Paul's
view here?

Paul's view of sin also seems to be rather confusing.
Romans 5:12–19 seems to say that we are sinners and judged
because of our sin in Adam. And yet in other passages Paul
said that we are judged because of our own personal sin
(Rom. 2:12–16). Indeed, Romans 5:12–14 says that sin is not
reckoned where there is no law, which presumably means
that sin is not accounted against one if there is no law pro-
hibiting a certain action. And then Paul said that there was no
law from the time of Adam until Moses. His argument seems
to be that people who lived in the interval between Adam and
Moses did not die because of their own sin but because they
sinned in Adam. This is supported by his argument that sin is
not reckoned when there is no law, and yet people died who
lived in the interval between Adam and Moses. Why did these
people die? Paul's argument in Romans 5:12–14 seems to be
that they died because of Adam's sin, not their own.

A problem arises, however, when we read Romans 2:12–16,
for there Paul said that those who sin without the law will
perish without the law. In Romans 2 his argument seems to
be that Gentiles will perish without the law because they have
sinned against the law of conscience. They were conscious of
a law within themselves even though the law was not written.
But if people without the law are judged by their observance
of an internal unwritten law, then what do we make of Paul's
statement in Romans 5:12ff. that sin is not reckoned where
there is no written law? Apparently sin is reckoned for Gentiles
who do not have Torah according to Romans 2.

My purpose here is not to provide solutions to the questions raised above, but rather to show that there are many difficult and important issues in Pauline theology that need
careful examination. Indeed, one can see from the examples
above why some scholars conclude that Pauline theology
lacks any coherence. But, as I have mentioned above, to
despair of seeing unity in Paul is to underestimate his intelli-
gence. One cannot unlock the mysteries of a complex thinker
without careful analysis.

Some Concluding Comments

Two final comments should be made about doing Pauline theology. First, some become suspicious of the validity of various solutions that are proposed because the solutions are carefully nuanced and must be stated with complexity. The objection I have heard is usually stated something like this: "The solution proposed is too sophisticated and complex to be credible. Paul was a simple, bold, and straightforward thinker. Involved and precise intellectual distinctions would have been repugnant to him." This objection, I think, is simply false. It assumes that real life is simple and straightforward and that nuanced distinctions are not important for practical living. As I have tried to indicate throughout this chapter, Paul was a sophisticated and complex thinker. Also, real life is incredibly complex and involved, and we have to make all kinds of careful distinctions in every area of life in order to live successfully.

Second, some of the tensions in Paul are so difficult to solve that one must finally appeal to the weight of the evidence in order to come to any resolution. In other words, one may incline toward one view rather than another because it answers more questions satisfactorily. Such solutions should not be dismissed simply because all contrary evidence cannot be explained in a satisfactory way. The issue is whether the solution offers the best solution in the light of the evidence we have. Scientific theories often do not answer all questions, but they are accepted as valid because they explain more of the evidence than any other theory. Certainly, one should continue searching for a theory that answers all remaining questions. However, it is quite legitimate to arrive at a conclusion without answering every possible question.

Pauline Theology in New Testament Scholarship

One's knowledge of Pauline theology can also be substantially increased by reading the work of scholars in this area. It is always helpful to see how others have wrestled with the same questions with which we are struggling. In addition, scholars can point out blind spots in our understanding, highlighting themes that we have missed completely in our own study. The reading of other scholars should provoke us to resume dialogue with Paul and ascertain whether the scholars have accurately represented Paul's theology.

The following is a brief list of some major theological works on Paul and biblical theology. An excellent place to begin is in works that provide a brief summary of Pauline theology.

J. A. Fitzmyer, *Paul and His Theology: A Brief Sketch*, 2d ed. (Englewood Cliffs, N.J.: Prentice-Hall, 1989).

J. Plevnik, *What Are They Saying About Paul?* (New York: Paulist, 1986).

J. A. Ziesler, *Pauline Christianity* (New York: Oxford University Press, 1983).

The student should not neglect reading the section on Paul in the major NT theologies.

R. Bultmann, *Theology of the New Testament*, 2 vols. (New York: Scribner's, 1951, 1955). Bultmann read Paul through the eyeglasses of existentialism. Nevertheless, his exposition of Pauline thought is brilliant and provocative.

H. Conzelmann, *An Outline of the Theology of the New Testament* (New York: Harper & Row, 1969). A useful concise work by a Bultmannian.

L. Goppelt, *Theology of the New Testament*, 2 vols. (Grand Rapids: Eerdmans, 1981, 1982). Volume two contains the discussion on Paul, which is insightful and helpful.

D. Guthrie, *New Testament Theology* (Downers Grove, Ill.: InterVarsity, 1981). This book borders on systematic rather than biblical theology, although Guthrie's thorough and careful analysis on Paul should be regularly consulted.

W. G. Kümmel, *The Theology of the New Testament According to Its Witnesses: Jesus–Paul–John* (Nashville: Abingdon, 1973). The section on Paul is brief but worth consulting.

G. E. Ladd, *A Theology of the New Testament* (Grand Rapids: Eerdmans, 1974). I still think this is the best theology of the NT. The section on Paul is lucid and stimulating. Written by an evangelical who adopts a salvation-historical perspective.

It is difficult to decide what to recommend from the works that are specifically on Paul. I have included books that I think are particularly stimulating or helpful.

J. C. Beker, *Paul the Apostle: The Triumph of God in Life and Thought* (Philadelphia: Fortress, 1980). Beker contended that apocalyptic is the center of Pauline thought in this innovative work.

W. D. Davies, *Paul and Rabbinic Judaism: Some Rabbinic Elements in Pauline Theology*, 4th ed. (Philadelphia: Fortress, 1980). Davies set forth the parallels between Paul's thinking and Rabbinic thought.

T. J. Deidun, *New Covenant Morality in Paul* (Rome: Biblical Institute Press, 1981). In my opinion, this is the best book in English on Pauline ethics and parenesis. He challenged and overturned many false conceptions about Pauline ethics.

J. Drane, *Paul, Libertine or Legalist? A Study of the Theology of the Major Pauline Epistles* (London: SPCK, 1975). A stimulating work that argues for a developmental schema in Paul's theology.

H. Hübner, *Law in Paul's Thought* (Edinburgh: T. & T. Clark, 1984). Another developmental view of Paul's thinking on the law. This is not an easy book to read.

S. Kim, *The Origin of Paul's Gospel* (Grand Rapids: Eerdmans, 1982). Kim traces the impact of the Damascus Road epiphany on Paul's theology.

J. Gresham Machen, *The Origin of Paul's Religion* (Grand Rapids: Eerdmans, 1978). This book should be still be read for its methodological rigor in exposing the weakness of the history of religions school.

R. P. Martin, *Reconciliation: A Study of Paul's Theology* (Atlanta: John Knox, 1981). Martin attempted to prove here that reconciliation is the center of Paul's theology.

D. Patte, *Paul's Faith and the Power of the Gospel: A Structural Introduction to the Pauline Letters* (Philadelphia: Fortress, 1983). This work investigates Pauline thought from a structuralist perspective.

H. Räisänen, *Paul and the Law* (Philadelphia: Fortress, 1986). A brilliant attempt to defend the thesis that Paul's thinking on the law is contradictory.

H. Ridderbos, *Paul: An Outline of His Theology* (Grand Rapids: Eerdmans, 1975). The most comprehensive and helpful single volume on Paul.

E. P. Sanders, *Paul, The Law, and the Jewish People* (Philadelphia: Fortress, 1983). Sanders, like Räisänen, also came to the conclusion that Paul's view of the law is not consistent.

_____, *Paul and Palestinian Judaism: A Comparison of Patterns of Religion* (Philadelphia: Fortress, 1977). A mold-breaking book in which Sanders challenges the thesis that Palestinian Judaism was legalistic.

H. J. Schoeps, *Paul: The Theology of the Apostle in the Light of Jewish Religious History* (Philadelphia: Westminster, 1961). A stimulating exposition of Pauline theology by a Jewish scholar.

F. Watson, *Paul, Judaism, and the Gentiles: A Sociological Approach* (New York: Cambridge University Press, 1986). A very provocative work that interprets Paul's stance on the law and the Gentiles from a sociological perspective.

S. Westerholm, *Israel's Law and the Church's Faith: Paul and His Recent Interpreters* (Grand Rapids: Eerdmans, 1988). This book contains a lucid exposition of the history of Pauline theology with respect to the law in the twentieth century. Westerholm also attempted to show that Luther's view on Paul was substantially on target.

The student of Paul should also consult works on biblical theology in general. Again, only a few works can be noted here.

B. S. Childs, *Biblical Theology in Crisis* (Philadelphia: Westminster, 1970). Childs introduced here his canonical perspective for doing theology.

O. Cullmann, *Salvation in History* (London: SCM, 1967). Cullmann has written several books on this theme but this is a helpful exposition of the salvation-historical position with responses to his critics.

J. D. G. Dunn, *Unity and Diversity in the New Testament: An Inquiry into the Character of Earliest Christianity* (Philadelphia: Westminster, 1977). A provocative book that explores many crucial issues for constructing a NT theology. Unfortunately, Dunn perceived a great deal of diversity but very little unity.

G. Hasel, *New Testament Theology: Basic Issues in the Current Debate* (Grand Rapids: Eerdmans, 1978). The best introductory volume to help the student chart his way in contemporary discussions of NT theology.

J. D. Smart, *The Past, Present and Future of Biblical Theology* (Philadelphia: Westminster, 1979). Smart disputed Childs' thesis (see above) in this work.

9

Delineating the Significance
of Paul's Letters

Old books are usually read because we think that those
books have something to say to contemporary life. This is
especially true of the Scriptures in general and the Pauline
letters in particular. It is fair to say, in fact, that the significance of the Pauline letters for today provokes such interest
in them. And that is how it should be. We study Paul because
we believe that through a keener understanding of Paul we
can hear the word of God in contemporary culture.

In this chapter we ask, How can or should we translate
Paul's message to the twentieth century? This question surfaces with even more intensity when the issue of cultural rela-
tivity is posed. What aspects of Paul's thought are applicable
to the twentieth century, and what features are limited to first
century culture, and thus should not be imposed on the
church today? The question of cultural limitation is particularly controversial, and I can only set forth what seems to be
the most reasonable position to me. Before we explore this
topic, however, a few words need to be said about the possibility of discerning the significance of Paul for today's world.

Can we discern and apply the significance of the Pauline
letters to contemporary culture? Or are we so entrapped in
our own cultural perspectives and historical background that
we inevitably understand the significance of Paul's letters in

151

terms of our own prejudices?[1] The danger of applying the significance of Scripture in terms of our own culture and prejudices is ever present. Nonetheless, if we are trapped in our culture then we are faced with hermeneutical nihilism. Experience teaches us that we can transcend our culture and hear and apply an alien word.

Some scholars think we should consciously adopt a bias when we read the Scriptures. They suggest that we should read Paul with a feminist bias[2], or with the assumption that God is on the side of the poor.[3] Such starting points guarantee that we will read our own culture into Paul. They ensure that as we read Paul we will see our own faces in the mirror. Instead, we should approach Paul with humble openness, prepared to hear even the most alien of words. We should be open to Paul being a feminist or a traditionalist or neither. What we want to discover is what Paul had to say. We should recognize that we are all inclined to read our own preconceptions into Paul, and thus we should struggle to read Paul on his own terms first and then apply his word to our culture.

Meaning and Significance

What is involved in applying the significance of Paul's writings to our own day? First of all, we need to distinguish between meaning and significance. Paul had a particular intended meaning in mind when he wrote his letters, and that meaning is unitary. The significance of a text, however, is manifold; it can apply to many situations.[4] When Paul said "do not be drunk with wine" (Eph. 5:18), he meant do not drink so much wine that you lose control of your mental capacities. The significance of this text has wider applications for today. What Paul said about drunkenness is a type that

1. For a discussion of issues of significance in biblical interpretation generally, see D. M. Scholer, "Issues in Biblical Interpretation," *Evangelical Quarterly* 88 (1988): 5–22. Scholer, in my opinion, was too pessimistic about our ability to transcend our own culture in applying the biblical text.

2. For this view, see E. S. Fiorenza, *In Memory of Her* (New York: Crossroad, 1983).

3. This is the tenet of much of liberation theology.

4. For this distinction, see E. D. Hirsch, Jr., *Validity in Interpretation* (New Haven: Yale University Press, 1967), 8. He developed this theme in a later essay entitled "Introduction: Meaning and Significance," in *Aims of Interpretation* (Chicago: University of Chicago Press, 1976), 1–13. P. D. Juhl (*Interpretation: An Essay in the Philosophy of Literary Criticism* [Princeton: Princeton University Press, 1980], 27–37, 226–30) identified a weakness in Hirsch's analysis of meaning and significance, but he showed that the distinction between meaning and significance is valid and crucial for interpretation.

applies to the use of any substance that causes one to surrender mental capacities. Thus, forbidding the use of mind altering drugs in order to "get high" would be a valid contemporary application of Ephesians 5:18.

Moving from Meaning to Significance

How do we move from the meaning of the Pauline letters to their significance? One way to do this is to formulate a principle from the passage under consideration. A principle is an abiding truth that deduces the general truth from the pericope under consideration. For example, the principle from Ephesians 5:18 could be "do not use any substance that will distort or alter your mental capacity in order to experience joy." It is too simplistic, however, to move directly from a principle to application to contemporary life because other factors must be taken into consideration. For example, one might deduce from 1 Corinthians 14:33b–36 that women should never speak in church, and one might conclude from 1 Corinthians 7 that one should never marry. Now both of these deductions are possible conclusions, but other factors must be taken into consideration before moving so quickly to the contemporary application of these texts.

What other factors need to be taken into consideration before applying the significance of Pauline texts to today? First, we need to recall again the occasional nature of the Pauline letters. Since Paul gave specific advice to his congregations as they struggled with specific problems, we cannot simply formulate a principle from a Pauline text and apply it to today without any further ado. His words regarding the silence of women and singleness cannot be understood without considering the particular situation that called forth these words. It seems that the women mentioned in 1 Corinthians 14 were creating some kind of disturbance in the church, and Paul reacted to this disorder in the community. He was not giving timeless advice for women in every conceivable situation. Paul's command for the women to be silent is not an absolute command that applies to all situations, but is a word that addresses a particular situation in Corinth. And Paul's commendation in 1 Corinthians 7 of the single state is partially a response to the Corinthians who seemed to prefer singleness. The Corinthians were exalting celibacy and in this chapter Paul established common ground with them, and also disagreed with some of their ideas on marriage and sexuality.

Second, we should not try to apply the significance of the Pauline letters without taking all of Pauline theology into account. Since Paul's letters are addressed to specific situations, one could get a lopsided picture of Paul's view on any issue if one merely consulted a single passage. That is why Pauline theology is such an important step in the exegetical process. It is not a step that drops out when one moves to significance or application!

Returning to our two examples, since Paul approved of women prophesying and praying in church in 1 Corinthians 11:2–16 (presuming Paul does not contradict himself), his word about women being silent in 1 Corinthians 14:33b–36 could not be an absolute word. A very exalted and noble view of marriage is presented in Ephesians 5:22–33, and thus it would be incorrect to conclude that Paul denigrated marriage in 1 Corinthians 7.

The importance of examining all of Paul's theology on a particular topic is apparent in other areas as well. We have indicated previously that it would be a mistake to derive the whole of Paul's view of the law from only the letter to the Galatians. Paul's theology of law in Galatians was partially a response to legalists who were overemphasizing the value of the law. Thus, Paul stressed liberation from law. On the other hand, we must be careful not to overlook what is contained in Galatians when we do formulate Paul's theology of law. Even though his words are occasional, it does not logically follow that they should be ignored in constructing Paul's view of the law. What he says in Galatians is part of his view of the law, and it must be integrated with what he says about the law elsewhere. It is inappropriate to wave the theology of law in Galatians aside and to concentrate only on what Paul says in Romans. The point is that we need to consider all of Paul's theology to construct his view of the topic in question. Such a process necessitates a serious consideration and fair integration of all the Pauline material.

Cultural Limitation

The necessity of consulting all of Paul's letters when synthesizing his theology of the law, his theology of the cross, or

his theology of the Spirit seems evident. We cannot understand the significance of Paul's words for today unless we
consult all of his letters for the fullest possible picture on each
of these topics. But the issue of cultural limitation in Paul's
writings has not yet been addressed. Paul's advice on women
may have been normative for his time, but surely his writings
have an element of cultural limitation, in which case not
everything he said is applicable to the contemporary world.
Paul commanded slaves to be obedient to their masters, and
yet no one believes that slavery is ordained of God. Very few
Christians believe that the holy kiss must be practiced in contemporary churches (1 Cor. 16:20). And should we all drink
wine when we have stomach aches just because Paul enjoined
Timothy to do so (1 Tim. 5:23)? Should women wear veils in
church (1 Cor. 11:2–16)? And do any churches follow Paul's
specific advice in 1 Timothy 5:3–16 about caring for widows?
Paul's strictures regarding the wearing of jewelry also seem to
be ignored (1 Tim. 2:9–10).

These examples should remind us that Paul wrote to a culture different from ours, and such differences need to be
taken into account. It would be culturally naive to try to
impose the world of the Bible onto contemporary culture.[5]
On the other hand, some writers have overemphasized the
cultural gap between the world of the Bible and today's world.
They have given the impression that the divide between the
world of the Bible and today is so large that the Bible cannot
speak to contemporary culture.[6] Most of the examples given
above are applicable to our culture if the distinction between
meaning and significance is maintained, and if one formu-
lates a principle from the passages in question.

The holy kiss need not be practiced in contemporary culture, but is there no word from God that can be applied to
our culture in this admonition? Certainly there is. The principle is that we should greet one another with fond affection in
Christ. Every culture has different ways of communicating
affection in a greeting, but the principle is that warm greetings should be shared in the Christian community. One does

5. Krister Stendahl warned of this danger in *The Bible and the Role of Women: A Case
Study in Hermeneutics* (Philadelphia: Fortress, 1966).
6. Stendahl in the book cited above falls into this trap. For a similar view, see D. E.
Nineham, *The Use and Abuse of the Bible: A Study of the Bible in an Age of Rapid Cultural
Change* (London: Macmillan, 1976).

not have to take wine when troubled with stomach pain, but the principle of the passage is quite timely for today. When one is sick, it is appropriate to take medicine to alleviate the pain. A liquid antacid may be just the cure! Unfortunately, some Christians today ignore Paul's advice from this passage and renounce the use of any medicine.

Paul wanted women to wear veils when prophesying, or wear their hair a certain way (the custom this passage is referring to is not clear) because the failure to abide by this custom confused the distinction between male and female and violated male headship. But in our culture the failure to wear veils does not indicate a confusion of the sexes nor does it communicate rebellion. In order to apply this passage to our culture we need to find customs or behaviors in our culture that would suggest androgyny or involve lack of submission to the order established by God.

No church follows Paul's specific advice to widows (1 Tim. 5:3–16), but it is hoped that churches do not ignore the principle of the passage. If a family cannot care for a widow, then the church should support her financially according to its ability. Paul's insistence that only those who truly are in financial need should be helped is also timely. The church that does nothing to help older people who have physical needs is a weak church indeed. In our culture today there is a bias against the old, and Paul's words here and in 1 Timothy 5:1–2 need to be recalled. Paul's advice regarding women's clothing and jewelry (1 Tim. 2:9–10) is often said to be inapplicable to our culture. Yet once again we can derive a very timely principle from this passage. The point of this passage is not to forbid the wearing of all jewelry (compare 1 Pet. 3:3, which, if taken literally, would seem to require no clothing at all!). Rather, Paul's aim here is to strike at materialism or sexual seduction. The women (this principle applies to men, too!) should not focus on clothing and jewelry, spending their financial resources on outer adornment. Their goal should be to cultivate godliness and to abound in good works. Surely, this is a powerful word for a materialistic and sexually perverted culture like ours.

What should we say, however, about Paul's instructions regarding slavery? We should point out that Paul nowhere recommended slavery as an institution. Instead, he *regulated* an institution that was already in existence. Nevertheless, his instructions on this topic indicate that Paul was not a believer in violent revolution. Obedience to the sphere in which one is called is the way of the gospel. The evils of such institutions are best cured by renewal from within rather than revolution from without.

Now it is also possible that Paul called on women to submit to their husbands (Eph. 5:22ff; Col. 3:18) and forbade them to teach men (1 Cor. 14:33b–36; 1 Tim. 2:11–15) because he was simply regulating common practices in those cultures. Thus, he called on husbands to lead with a loving authority. Or perhaps Paul did not call for changes in relations between men and women because such changes would cast aspersions on the message of the gospel, and thereby lead other people in Greco-Roman culture to reject the gospel message.[7] Paul would never exalt the liberation of women over the progress of the gospel, and the people in that culture were simply not ready to hear Paul's radical message of liberation.

Another possibility is that we should adopt a developmental hermeneutic in interpreting Paul's statements on women.[8] The focus should be on redemption in Christ rather than on creation; the stress should be on how Jesus treated women and Galatians 3:28 rather than the limitations that are placed on women. According to this approach, these limitations are due to the circumstances of the NT period, but the central hermeneutical texts proclaim redemption, liberty, and equality between the sexes.

On the other hand, some scholars think that Paul's limitations on women are still normative today.[9] They point out that Paul argued from creation for the distinctions between men and women (1 Cor. 11:7ff.; 1 Tim. 2:11–15). The appeal to creation to justify the distinction in roles between men and women indicates that Paul was not simply regulating a cultural norm of his day. Instead, Paul thought that such distinc-

7. For a defense of this view, see Alan Padgett, "The Pauline Rationale for Submission: Biblical Feminism and the *hina* Clauses of Titus 2:1–10," *Evangelical Quarterly* 59 (1987): 39–52.

8. Suggested by Richard Longenecker in his book, *New Testament Social Ethics for Today* (Grand Rapids: Eerdmans, 1984), and his article "Authority, Hierarchy & Leadership Patterns in the Bible," in *Women, Authority & the Bible*, ed. A. Mickelsen (Downers Grove, Ill.: InterVarsity, 1986), 66–85.

9. Probably the best defense of this view is found in J. B. Hurley's, *Man and Woman in Biblical Perspective* (Grand Rapids: Zondervan, 1981).

tions were fundamentally rooted in the way God created men and women. Neither, they say, is it logically satisfying to separate creation from redemption, since creation was not flawed but good from the beginning. In this view distinctions in role do not obliterate the equality in essence between men and women because Paul can argue in the same context both for the differences in role and the fundamental equality between men and women (1 Cor. 11:7–12). He apparently did not see any contradiction in affirming both of these simultaneously.

How does the modern reader decide which one of these two positions is correct? Arbitrating this issue is not my goal here, for that would put us in a very long and complex discussion.[10] What I want to do is to formulate some principles that ought to be considered before one comes to a conclusion.

First, all of Paul's teaching on women should be considered. Paul affirmed the equality of men and women in Christ (Gal. 3:28), and he also acknowledged that women had prophetic gifts and were involved in ministry (e.g., 1 Cor. 11:5; Phil. 4:2–3). Yet he also placed a limitation on women speaking in church (1 Cor. 14:33b–36; 1 Tim. 2:11–15). No resolution is satisfactory that does not explain all of the evidence in Paul.

Second, some scholars have claimed that in interpreting Paul's significance for today one must choose as one's starting point either Galatians 3:28 or the passages that limit women.[11] In principle this methodological starting point is possible, for clear texts should inform obscure texts. But the interpreter must be very careful that modern sensitivities and views do not rule on this issue. It is possible that Paul thought that both emphases were compatible and logically consistent. We may also have a tendency to label passages as obscure that are distasteful to us.

Third, in my opinion, the crucial issue is whether Paul's limitations on women are fully explicable from the specific situations that Paul addressed. If Paul limited women solely

10. My own view is expressed in two essays: "The Valuable Ministries of Women in the Context of Male Leadership in the Church," and "1 Corinthians 11:2–16: Head Coverings, Prophecies, and the Trinity," in *Recovering Biblical Manhood and Womanhood*, ed. W. Grudem and J. Piper (Westchester, Ill.: Crossway, forthcoming).

11. Paul K. Jewett (*Man as Male and Female* [Grand Rapids: Eerdmans, 1976]) argued explicitly for the incompatibility of Paul's view of women in his book. He said that the modern person should accept Galatians 3:28 as the authoritative view on women for today.

because of specific problems and abuses that arose in the churches, then his words of limitation are not a principle that should apply today. The principle for today would be that we should not allow false teaching, uneducated teachers, or lack of order and propriety in contemporary churches. On the other hand, if Paul argued from creation, then Paul's teaching on the limitation of women still applies today because in this case Paul was basing his view on the way God intended life to be lived from the beginning. If this latter view is true, then Paul's limitation does not stem from the fall but precedes the fall.

To sum up, one delineates the significance of Paul's letters for today by (1) formulating a principle from the passage; (2) consulting all of the Pauline teaching on the issue; (3) constructing his teaching into a unified whole; and (4) determining whether Paul's advice is solely explicable from the specific situation he addressed or whether it stems from God's intention in creation.

We should add that the interpreter still has much work to do even after discovering the general principle for today's world. The interpreter must ask, How does this principle apply in today's world? Inevitably, people who agree on the basic principle sometimes disagree on the specific application of that principle. The application of biblical truth to contemporary situations can be extraordinarily complex. Such complexity should lead us to humility as we try to apply the principles of the Pauline letters to our contemporary world.

Conclusion

We have come to the end of our investigation into how one should interpret the Pauline letters. A brief summary of the various steps is appropriate here.

1. The student must understand the nature of letters before he or she begins to interpret the Pauline letters. The literary form of the letter in general should be identified, and any particular literary features should be observed. The interpreter should also keep in mind that Paul's letters are usually occasional responses to specific problems in the churches. A clearer understanding of each letter will be possible if the interpreter cautiously reconstructs the situation or problem in the community to which Paul wrote. Naturally, the student will not be able to reconstruct the situation of the letter before doing an exegesis of the letter.

2. The student should then investigate any text-critical variants in the passage or letter being investigated so that the correct text for exegesis may be analyzed. The student should also note any text-critical variants that reveal how others interpreted the passage.

3. Of course, step one cannot be carried out until the student prepares a translation of the text and identifies every form that occurs.

4. In this step the student examines historical and introductory issues. Delving into historical issues has two

facets. First, the student gains as much knowledge as possible of the Greco-Roman world and Jewish culture. Second, the student should research any particular cultural features (such as the "girding of loins") that occur in the text. The examination of introductory issues helps the student gain some awareness of the views of critical scholarship on the letter under consideration. Issues such as authenticity, the date of the letter, the integrity of the letter, and the identity of the adversaries are usually discussed. The student should begin to form his or her own position on these issues after interacting with critical scholarship. Of course, the conclusions of the student may be refined or changed after completing an intensive exegesis of the entire letter.

5. The fifth step begins an intensive analysis of the text itself by conducting a grammatical analysis. This involves the diagramming of the text and the identification of the grammatical function of each word in the text.

6. After diagramming the text the student is prepared to trace the argument of the text. Only by explaining the function of every proposition in the Pauline letters can the student attain enlightenment. Enlightenment means that the student not only understands what Paul said, but he or she can explain the structure of that argument to others.

7. Part of the hermeneutical circle, of course, is that propositions cannot be understood without understanding the individual words that form the sentences. Lexical study, then, is crucial for a grasp of the Pauline argument. Students should be particularly sensitive to the fact that words in Paul form part of the profile that results in Pauline theology.

8. Theological synthesis is an essential part of Pauline exegesis. The student asks how the conclusions obtained in this passage harmonize with other Pauline teachings. If a resolution cannot be found between the particular passage under investigation and Pauline teaching elsewhere, then three possibilities present themselves (assuming Paul does not contradict himself): (1) the interpretation of the passage under consideration coheres

with the rest of the Pauline teaching, but the student
does not yet understand *how* it harmonizes with the rest
of his teaching; (2) the student has misunderstood what
Paul teaches elsewhere, and such teaching must now be
qualified or discarded in the light of what has been discovered during exegesis; or (3) the student has misunderstood the particular passage which he has studied.
The clear teaching of Paul elsewhere summons the student to reexamine the validity of his or her interpretation of the passage under consideration.

9. Last, the significance of the Pauline teaching for today
is probed. I have stressed that the contemporary significance of Scripture is what drives all of exegesis. We
strive to hear the voice of God both for our own lives
and for the life of the church in the world. The Holy
Spirit enables us to apply the words of the text to our
own situation, and thereby we are strengthened and
encouraged to carry out God's work in the world.

Select Commentaries
on the Pauline Epistles

Bibliographical recommendations have been made throughout the course of the book, but nothing has been said about commentaries. To select the three most useful commentaries on each Pauline letter for students is not an easy task. Nonetheless, my recommendations for the Pauline letters follow.

Romans

J. D. G. Dunn, *Romans*, Word Biblical Commentary, 2 vols. (Waco, Tex.: Word, 1988).

C. E. B. Cranfield, *A Critical and Exegetical Commentary on the Epistle to the Romans*, International Critical Commentary, 2 vols. (Edinburgh: T. & T. Clark, 1975, 1979).

E. Käsemann, *Commentary on Romans* (Grand Rapids: Eerdmans, 1980).

1 Corinthians

C. K. Barrett, *A Commentary on the First Epistle to the Corinthians*, Harper's New Testament Commentaries (New York: Harper & Row, 1968).

H. Conzelmann, *1 Corinthians: A Commentary on the First Epistle to the Corinthians*, Hermeneia (Philadelphia: Fortress, 1975).

G. D. Fee, *1 Corinthians*, New International Commentary on the New Testament (Grand Rapids: Eerdmans, 1987).

2 Corinthians

C. K. Barrett, *A Commentary on the Second Epistle to the Corinthians*, Harper's New Testament Commentaries (New York: Harper & Row, 1973).

V. P. Furnish, *II Corinthians*, Anchor Bible (Garden City: Doubleday, 1984).

P. E. Hughes, *Paul's Second Epistle to the Corinthians*, New International Commentary on the New Testament (Grand Rapids: Eerdmans, 1962).

Galatians

H. D. Betz, *Galatians: A Commentary on Paul's Letter to the Churches in Galatia*, Hermeneia (Philadelphia: Fortress, 1979).

F. F. Bruce, *Commentary on Galatians*, New International Greek Testament Commentary (Grand Rapids: Eerdmans, 1982).

E. D. Burton, *A Critical and Exegetical Commentary on the Epistle to the Galatians*, International Critical Commentary (Edinburgh: T. & T. Clark, 1920).

Ephesians

M. Barth, *Ephesians*, Anchor Bible, 2 vols. (Garden City: Doubleday, 1974).

F. F. Bruce, *The Epistles to the Colossians, to Philemon and to the Ephesians*, New International Commentary on the New Testament (Grand Rapids: Eerdmans, 1984).

C. L. Mitton, *Ephesians*, New Century Bible Commentary (Grand Rapids: Eerdmans, 1981).

Philippians

G. F. Hawthorne, *Philippians*, Word Biblical Commentary (Waco, Tex.: Word, 1983).

R. P. Martin, *Philippians*, New Century Bible Commentary (Grand Rapids: Eerdmans, 1980).

M. Silva, *Philippians*, Wycliffe Exegetical Commentary (Chicago: Moody, 1988).

Colossians-Philemon

E. Lohse, *Colossians-Philemon: A Commentary on the Epistles to the Colossians and Philemon*, Hermeneia (Philadelphia: Fortress, 1971).

C. F. D. Moule, *The Epistles of Paul the Apostle to the Colossians and to Philemon*, Cambridge Greek Testament Commentary (Cambridge: Cambridge University Press, 1957).

P. T. O'Brien, *Colossians, Philemon*, Word Biblical Commentary (Waco, Tex.: Word, 1982).

1-2 Thessalonians

E. Best, *A Commentary on the First and Second Epistles to the Thessalonians*, Harper's New Testament Commentaries (New York: Harper & Row, 1972).

F. F. Bruce, *1 & 2 Thessalonians*, Word Biblical Commentary (Waco, Tex.: Word, 1982).

I. H. Marshall, *1 and 2 Thessalonians*, New Century Bible Commentary (Grand Rapids: Eerdmans, 1983).

Pastorals

M. Dibelius and H. Conzelmann, *The Pastoral Epistles: A Commentary on the Pastoral Epistles*, Hermeneia (Philadelphia: Fortress, 1972).

G. D. Fee, *1 & 2 Timothy, Titus*, Good News Commentary (San Francisco: Harper & Row, 1984; revised, NIBC, 1988).

J. N. D. Kelly, *A Commentary on the Pastoral Epistles: I Timothy, II Timothy, Titus*, Harper's New Testament Commentaries (New York: Harper & Row, 1963).